ASSESSING THE
CHARACTER
OF CANDIDATES FOR
NATIONAL POLITICAL
OFFICE

In Search of a Collaborative Spirit

Gordon J. Hilsman, D. Min.

Assessing the CHARACTER of Candidates for National Political Office:

In Search of a Collaborative Spirit

Gordon J Hilsman websites:

www.gordonjhilsman.com

www.spiritualclinician.com

Dedication

To my father, Arthur, blue-collar worker, obscure citizen, no high school diploma, and the best man I ever met.

Disclaimer

If I were to confess all my life failures in this book, it would likely sell better. But exaggerations of our transgressions and omissions are no humbler than minimizing or hiding them. If this book sounds haughty in places, forgive me. Who, after all, can accurately judge the character of another (Twitter or X aside!)? Most of the convictions of this writing came from recognizing my own failures of character to show up when needed most, some after I turned seventy.

Commenting on the character of public figures takes on the added vulnerability of the inherent mystery of the spaces where sacred privacy intermingles with public responsibility. More than any other public responsibility, the leadership of nations needs checks and balances. If top political leaders do not have at least a modicum of essential characteristics, they are a chef poisoning hundreds of patrons or a kind, spindly boy quarterbacking an NFL championship game. By assessing the character of top leaders, we do what we can to protect society and give it direction for future excellence.

Author's Preface

This book is for voters: those who already believe that people who hold national political positions should possess solid character to qualify. These pages may also be instructive for others, but this book is intended to provide a bit of guidance for adults beginning to take seriously the character of political candidates vying to fill national elected offices. This writing contributes to one theme of evolution that recounts the historical thinking of citizens, or at least the writers among them, about what characteristics are necessary for beneficially serving entire nations in top leadership. Rather than inspecting candidates for what is wrong with them, it suggests new ways to quasi-clinically identify the best candidates for serving as national leaders.

As a mostly good Catholic boy, I once realized that I was more fascinated by the notion of virtue than anybody around me. The same seemed true in theology school on my way to ten years as a Catholic priest. But virtue took on a new meaning during my two years as chaplain-counselor in a Chicago alcoholism treatment facility where it became obvious that without specific observable virtues, former patients generally failed to maintain sobriety for very long. They used more colloquial words than those we have from history, but the mix of key characteristics – everyday radical *honesty*, richly and often felt *gratefulness*, near-heroic *courage*, and a new kind of stark *humility*, proved essential to continuing recovery. Rigorous *self-monitoring*, working to free oneself of past *regrets and resentments*, and active *care of other people* also emerged as essential. A*nd these characteristics were partially visible!* As lenses through which to view people, they were instructive of their character. Little had I known as a clergyperson that those virtues I'd learned so early in life were deeply functional for recovery from addiction. (See Chapter Three and Chapter Four).

What I learned about character from that Chicago initiation was repeated over and over in the small process group clinical education programs I led for over 40 years in hospital systems across the country, from Massachusetts General to the University of Southern California Hospital, Los Angeles County, and mostly in the northern Midwest and Pacific Northwest. Such groups are interpersonally rigorous and vigorous, compelling group members to engage in dynamic sessions with five or six peers, giving and receiving stark feedback to each other to expand self-awareness and competence in engaging patients of all kinds in open, tense, and often painful depth. There again were those virtues, unnamed most of the time, but essential: interpersonal courage, care of other people that meticulously observed and challenged for improvement, stark honesty, and willingness to confront one another for our own good and identified personal and interpersonal goals for change.

All of this has been unexpected preparation for the communal task of assessing the character of candidates for public political office. Such a practice, if widely applied during political campaigns and elections, would be neither neat nor foolproof. But over time, voters learning to think about and challenge candidates' character reasonably well could transform our government. As we voters become convinced that character matters and get more practiced at identifying specific personal characteristics as indicators of the collaborative spirit necessary to govern successfully, we will be replacing mediocre and incompetent leaders with far more effective ones. This book begins preparing voters for that long-term task.

Character assessment is not a moral judgment. It is a pragmatic description of positive attributes that make it more likely that a person will have success at contributing to the human community. It fits better in spiritual theology, what is beautiful, than in moral theology, what is bad or wrong. Colloquially, there are three branches of theology: 1) what is, 2) What should be, and 3) What should not be. Character assessment fits best in what should be or what is elegant, effective, and positive for humanity.

The reader will find in these pages no use of the names of major political parties. Using those names *in any way* now perpetuates the dualistic partisanship that is defeating our collaborative government process. So many powerful and nasty assumptions now accompany those party names that their very use derails issues and stagnates discussion. To function somewhat consistently in the best interest of the people, our leaders all need to be quit of the incessant blaming, intentional obfuscating, manipulative maneuvering, and coercive powering that now distract them from consistently collaborating on finding the best policy and program efforts at fashioning potential solutions for constituents' needs.

Assessing leaders' character is not new, although previously, it has been done almost entirely informally, in a paucity or words. But for at least a few thousand years that we know of, some citizens have been pondering and writing about the unfairness and even depravity of top leaders, yearning for a way to find quality leadership. Yearning and creative people eventually developed words to describe what they yearned for in their top leaders: politically interested, strong, and bright people who are at least adequate to the leadership task, with reasonable cognition and a smidgen of fairness. We put that slice of evolution into Chapter Two of this book by following a brief history of the development of virtue in several parts of the world.

No doubt, over the course of millennia, there are other great unnamed contributors to that character-pondering thread of recent evolution than those reported on here. The author couldn't research them all. But coalescing the virtue concepts of historically great thinkers as the language of character, even to the limited degree of this book, suggests a way to discuss the viability of potential top leaders of a great pluralistic country that is only vaguely and sporadically seeing the need to struggle for a collaborative spirit among them. This kind of character assessment is long overdue. Our hope must be that it is not too late.

Table Of Contents

Chapter One:

The Political Need to Look Closely at Character

The hyper-partisan milieu in national politics is now so deep and widespread that no organizational change will fix it, even a constitutional congress. Over time, it will take a brand-new process that pays more attention to the basic character of those elected to top positions. That development must be accomplished by voters and leaders who possess a genuine collaborative spirit to organize it and demand it.

The character of our citizenry and our national leaders matters far more than their charisma and attractiveness and at least as much as their political stances. Lack of quality character pervades our society. To change the course of an entire population, however, is too mammoth a project. Since we all tend to see the character of other people more clearly than our own, we can benefit from looking first at the character of our top leaders. As my old hospital administrator used to say, "There are always problems, and they are always people." Or Shakespeare's Julius Caesar, "Our problems, my dear Brutus, are not in our stars but in ourselves."

To reduce the fetters of the intense political dualism we call partisanship, the chief cluster of characteristics to assess in candidates for elections now constitutes a *collaborative spirit*. A major portion of the cause of gridlock *is inside the leaders*. Spirit is the elan of a given person, the liveliness, the unique values, habits, and patterns of relating that makeup that person. Without a collaborative spirit, top leaders simply go their own way, following distractions around which they splinter. The way out of gridlock is not only in changing structure but being more careful about the character of those we elect.

The overall question in our minds must be, "Does this person possess the character – enough of that array of positive traits that will compel them from the inside to consistently work together for the complex needs of the public interest – or not?"

Yes, *positive* characteristics. Those are much more difficult to recognize than nasty criticisms using invectives and vituperations. And more crucial. They signal character.

How can we begin that long process of replacing dualistic and fiercely partisan leaders with those in possession of a collaborative spirit? Voters will need to assess their character before we elect them. Eventually, we will need to show the media and party leaders how valuable it is to attend to candidates' character.

From the Greek, the word character means "something cut or engraved into a hard substance that makes it unique and distinguishable from other similar artifacts." It refers to a mark made to last. Applied to descriptions of persons, it is *an array of distinct, positive qualities that make that person uniquely valuable, a person among persons, set apart by expectations of quality.*

It can also refer to quirky qualities as in, "That guy's a real *character!*" In assessing candidates, the word could be used in either or both senses, referring to sets of relatively enduring positive relational habits, traits, or qualities. Everyone has some character. It is its blend of sensitivity with toughness that matters-- intelligence with directed passion, substance and depth with flexibility, and imaginative creativity that can be described as so highly beneficial in top leaders.—

A collaborative spirit can be described as *a liveliness for working together with diverse others to consistently improve effective shared decision-making*. Such a life attitude is a matter of character, not only eloquence, charisma, financial backing, or rhetoric. It emanates from inside a person, wrought almost mystically by birth assets and past important life experiences, both those perceived as successful on the one hand and those felt as failures on the other. Such a spirit is no doubt shaped by observing respected others' impressive behavior in relationships; learning in youth and later from inspiring stories and teachings in schools, teams, and churches; and by scores of other experiences that we can never measure.

As a cluster of characteristics, a collaborative spirit bends people towards internal joyfulness and external enthusiasm for self-improvement as a team or project committee member. It makes one stretch time, energy, and attention, and it is invested in persistently making contributions, however crucial or tiny, to the betterment of humanity. It cannot be described in a sound bite or catchy phrase. It is a combination of many developed capacities that, while they do not make a person perfect, they do make them at least viable as quality citizens and top working leaders.

It has been reported by at least a few former congresspersons that they entered politics with the enthusiasm and even idealism of a raw collaborative spirit but left that endeavor surprisingly soon, discouraged by the lack of such a spirit in the collective of colleagues in that milieu. Such a spirit of working together needs partners. Otherwise, it is like a child at the playground with nobody her size around, wanting to play but unable to find anybody to join her.

Currently, in the U.S., there is no known formal effort to consider the character of candidates in assessing them for national government positions. Is that not ridiculous? Candidates might not even be asked officially about their history of use of mood-altering substances, mental illness, or prior accusations of sexual impropriety. It appears to voters that candidates' privilege has already begun at candidacy. It is quickly frowned upon to ask penetrating questions about character, even though within months, that aspiring leader may well be representing millions of people, charged and well compensated for working diligently to preserve and improve people's lives and living conditions.

Are a candidate's character strengths and weaknesses not relevant to their receiving voters' enormous trust?

Despite advancements in personal helping relationships of the past century and copious psychological, management, and leadership development writing, we still make our decisions about who will lead us in congress and the administration by such outmoded measures as how much money they can raise for their campaign, how well they can dominate others in 75 second TV debate speeches, how faithful they are to current political party priorities, and how they appear in slick public relations videos. What about their values, their verve, their character as human beings? Isn't a character, or lack of it, what wanes so thoroughly when top national leaders take their countries all the way to combat and near bankruptcy almost on their own?

With concerted effort, voters can now make assessments of character early, before or during election campaigns, to better inform our decisions on whom to vote. That may sound naïve but in the vital task of extricating our country from massive dualistic gridlock is based on the conviction that eventually composing a workable government that can respond nimbly to the rapidly changing needs of a huge pluralistic nation in a technologically complex age will require a preponderance of individuals who have the character necessary to do so.

We are not the first to face this project of finding adequately virtuous leaders. There is a strain of history that has recorded scraps of the yearning for better top leaders for centuries. For example, an entire literary genre now called "Mirrors for Princes" that was common between 700 and 1530 AD consisted of letters, notes, treatises, and other advisory writing that chided princes (government leaders) to look at themselves as their subjects were seeing them, and behave with greater respect for their citizens. The later, common children's story, *The Emperor's New Clothes* (C.A. Reitzel, 1837) pointedly and amusingly makes the same point. Learning to assess politicians' character begins with a quick look at that process of forging humility (self-understanding and image awareness) into top leaders. The language for that new self-insight is that of character, historically often in some cultures using the words of virtues.

That language of virtue was referred to by some early American leaders, including James Madison, in the Federalist Papers:

The aim of every political constitution is, or ought to be, first to obtain for rulers, men [sic] who possess most wisdom to discern, and most virtue to pursue the common good of the society; and in the next place, to take the most effectual precautions for keeping them virtuous whilst they continue to hold their public trust. [iii]

Taking that mandate seriously, we quickly find that the entire process of leader selection today is highly flawed. It overtly ignores the character of candidates. The notion of virtue seems to have become suspect, seen perhaps as more Catholic than simply human or pragmatic. Now, with major developments in society, in business, in psychology, and in political science, we are poised to take another step in how we choose our leaders. The language of virtue can work for the assessment of character.

Currently, we voters are restricted by party leaders' ridiculously shallow procedures that essentially tell us nothing at all about the personal depths of our final candidates. Party leaders heavily manage election processes, and they either don't yet know how to assess character or don't make the character of candidates a priority at all. They seem almost desperately to want their party to win politically, for their own public survival and life satisfaction, as well as presumably to do what they think is the best for our national society. But when they are aware of difficult characteristics in a candidate, they are likely to suppress knowledge of those defects to optimize the likelihood that that candidate will be elected anyway. We are then left with some of our top leaders of a powerful and wealthy country making outrageously faulty statements in public, refusing or unable to talk seriously and cogently about key issues, and even vigorously proclaiming and selling conspiracy theories that have repeatedly been proven false. Brash offensive hyperbole, defensive minimizing, reflexive blaming, and congenial obfuscating can occasionally now win the day and the office.

Granted, there are so far only a few national leaders who act so outrageously. But citizens seem to agree that hyper-partisanship, entitlement status, and self-interest abound among our top leaders, hamstring their overall careful, concerted focus on the nation's needs. Character? It seems to be considered out of bounds to question it. But now we must.

The original meaning of the term politics – *the science of good sense applied to public affairs* – no longer seems to fit much of our national government at all. Selecting candidates for national leadership now must include them being challenged about elements of their deeper character, preferably even before they are admitted into candidacy. There is no viable substitute for a measure of emotional and behavioral maturity in national leaders.

Some good news is that character can now be assessed. In recent years, writers have sought ways of assessing several aspects of potential presidents to predict which candidate will make a viable one. James David Barber (The Presidential Character: Predicting Performance in the White House, 2021) has been writing about presidents for decades regarding various skills and knowledge it takes to be a successful president. And more recently, celebrated political scientist Gautam Mukunda has used political science, psychology, organizational behavior, and economics in Picking Presidents: How to Make the Most Consequential Decision in the World (2022) to suggest ways voters can predict the unpredictable— which candidate will become a successful president.

But if character is the central problem for finding excellent or even adequate political leaders, then discerning a collaborative spirit based on possession of its key virtues will be a window on candidates that ought not to be left out. And it is not only the president who needs to be assessed. Congresspersons too.

How then shall we appraise them? One thing is certain: It will need to be by brand-new components to the process of candidate selection.

Character assessment can't be done easily, nor thoroughly, nor infallibly. But it can be done usefully, confidently, and far more accurately than with any current assessment processes we make by glances, gossip, prepared videos, and hyperbolic social media touting or criticism.

Three barriers to candid character assessment of political candidates will need to be overcome: 1) Lack of a language, an organized collection of named characteristics with which to converse about character; 2) Lack of a forum in which candidates can be encountered about their character and receive quality interpersonal feedback on how they are seen by savvy constituents; and 3) Lack of an organized process and skilled constituents ready and willing to challenge candidates about the highly personal arena of their character.

Beginning to inquire about the collaborative character of applicants early will be a start. Even bringing focus to candidates' attention on their own character will improve the quality of our national leadership by influencing who will run. It is likely to be a different kind of person who will commit to running for national office. Some of those applicants of lesser character may walk away fearing exposure. Others who have been waiting for more good sense in campaigns and governing may then get involved anew in politics. When they see there is the hope of working alongside people who maintain a genuine collaborative spirit, seriously humanistic people may "come out of the woodwork."

Quality character is partially visible. It is thus possible to prod it to come forth more boldly when it is facilitated and confronted. That soft but tough confrontation approach can now proceed, along with closer observation of candidates' behavior in public presentations, to give us hints about their character. A new process, using small group encounter with eye-to-eye confrontation by real citizens can eventually be added as we will describe in Chapter Six.

But first we must look at the history of the development of character language, that quiet wave of evolutionary progress that has made us now ready with criteria for assessment of character.

Chapter Two:

Character Language Evolving

The practice of using observations about a person's character to gradually improve human leadership and citizenship has evolved.

In the 18 century BCE, when Hammurabi and his neighbors began to devise writing aimed at regulating peoples' society-damaging behavior, they were initiating what would be a long process of activity to improve character for communal living. Only later, roughly two millennia did the word virtue be used at all to identify specific capacities needed for people to live together and be governed effectively.

Like most lines of evolution, virtue's development has had a spotty, diverse, and intermittent history. Citizens and thinkers in various cultures in several places on the planet have been yearning and striving for leadership that is protective, effective, and especially just. Seldom have they found it. That enigmatic core of human evolution continues today all over the world. Chances are it will for a long time to come.

Human decisions do influence the path of evolution now that the evolutionary process itself has bequeathed to us the minds and hearts able to make decisions that contribute to it. What we do to identify leaders with character will be contributing to evolution's path, eventually to an enduring and enjoyable global community. That makes virtue assessment pragmatic – it has a highly significant purpose.

Virtue is essentially the evolving language of humanity to evaluate people's positive qualities as human beings, and particularly as leaders. As such, the language of virtue has always been pragmatic, not merely religious or aesthetic. It has been people-centered, in a strain of humanism winding around, within, above, and without religion. It has arisen from citizens' yearning more and more for compassion, understanding, fairness and help; from their seeing positive character sadly and painfully absent in people with power; and from their observing it as surprisingly abundant and appealing in a few great leaders.

The language of virtue has grown due to people responding to painful human situations to find better ways of communal living. Not always well understood, it grew with needing to decide which tribal member to trust, which neighbor to work with, and later, which applicant to hire, and which policeperson or clergyperson to avoid. Now, the focus needs to be on which aspiring political candidate to vote for. Dedication to assessing virtue and the use of it for specific purposes is still fledgling, but it continues to develop.

The word virtue in recent centuries still evokes thoughts and feelings of religion and may be rejected by some people along with the worst of religious history. The key historical figures developing virtue language so gradually, however, are not all religious or spiritual leaders. Among the contributors to the evolving body of virtue language were Hammurabi, a king; Plato, a philosopher; Pierre Teilhard de Chardin, a paleontologist; and Confucius. a teacher. Virtue is not only a religious word but a human one.

Hammurabi (c.1810 - 1750 BCE, Iraq)

One of the first attempts to identify and promote positive characteristics of people was verbalized by Hammurabi, a son of a king and eventually a king himself, whose key preserved thinking is etched on a 7-foot (2.25 m.) diorite stele originally found buried south of Baghdad in 1901 and now viewed at the Louvre in Paris. He was seeking to promote a semblance of justice with a novice first attempt at using law to improve the community.

The Code of Hammurabi is widely recognized as one of the earliest written efforts to make statements that might identify and curtail the nasty behavior of people in their relationships with one another. It was the result of a young King of Mesopotamia reflecting on, deciding about, and codifying, in its 282 briefly stated fledgling laws, indirectly revealing peoples' pain from the often brutal, reactive, and vindictive treatment of each other. They were yearning for fairness, though they seem to have had no word for it yet. They apparently felt the hurt of injustice inside their hearts often. The code shows how people began seeking more reliable safety from one another in their efforts at communal living. Maybe there were other virtues, courage and mercy perhaps, being generated and passed on orally earlier by evolving communities [iv] in other countries. But justice, though not named at the time, was clearly one of the first virtues represented in written words.

Hammurabi seems to have been a remarkable man, a step or two advanced beyond his time. We can imagine that he was more sensitive than those around him. He grew up feeling the hurt of people. There must have been a time when he had a bold realization that behaviors such as lying, theft, bullying, and romantic infidelity hurt people so commonly that it made life chaotic and chronically painful for everybody. Just past the vague animal awareness of pack benefits in hunting, they were reflexively interacting largely for their own individual benefit. That had lasted for thousands of years. But Hammurabi's experience was different, a breakthrough towards sporadic caring virtue.

He saw that fear abounded everywhere. Hostility, sneakiness, theft, and domination of women were the way of the world. Conceptualization was not yet widespread in human evolution at the time, so the code is highly concrete. The name and verbal conceptualizations of the virtue of justice, the code's primary theme, were to come later. But Hammurabi had seen the roots of them already.

Some psychological and personality theory writers neglect the emotion of *hurt* when identifying basic emotions felt by people as human beings, regardless of their culture of origin and development. The lists of universal emotions commonly include fear, anger, sadness, joy, and sometimes regret (guilt/shame). Leaving out hurt seems painfully unfortunate. Hurt is central to the human experience. It is the unsettled twinge of inner pain that commonly accompanies people witnessing their own or someone else's physical, interpersonal, and emotional misfortune, including at being treated badly by other people. Hurt is what we avoid in fear, retaliate from in anger, sense when we remember our own actions of hurting those we love, and nurse ourselves from sadness. Hammurabi responded to that hurt without ever naming it. It probably had no name in his native Akkadian[v].

The Code of Hammurabi was brutal to today's sensibilities, with personal hurt ubiquitous in both the proscribed behavior and its punishments. The penalties listed along with most of the stated infractions, were severe. The king apparently thought he needed to get the attention of a savage, near-animal society and was thinking that fear might do that. The code contains such identified unacceptable behaviors as stated in its first law, "If a man brings [sic] an accusation against a man, and charge him with a (capital) crime, but cannot prove it, he, the accuser, shall be put to death." Another, number 157, states that "If a man lies in the bosom of his mother after (the death of) his father, they shall burn both of them." The consequences for what was commonly seen as injustice or destructive to the community were drastic. Dozens of the penalties were to be put to death, and dozens more were to be thrown into the river, presumably to be put in peril of their life if they could not swim. The river currents would decide if they were evil or just unfortunate.

Hammurabi seems to have thought the violence among the ancients needed considerable pain in punishment to curtail it. That was brutal but more effective than today's courts which often seem to overlook the punishment of the wealthy and powerful. (Would a few lashes, cut-off fingers, and throws in the river be more effective for today's elite entitled?)

Here is the origin of "an eye for an eye", though Hammurabi probably didn't author it himself as a principle in his day.

196. If a man destroys the eye of another man, they shall destroy his eye.

197. If one breaks a man's bone, they shall break his bone.

198. If one destroys the eye of a freeman or breaks the bone of a freeman, he shall pay one mana of silver.

199. If one destroys the eye of a man's slave or breaks the bone of a man's slave, he shall pay one-half his price.

200. If a man knocks out a tooth of a man of his own rank, they shall knock out his tooth.

W. If one knocks out a tooth of a freeman, he shall pay one -third mana of silver.

Still, there are several of the 282 laws that show considerable mercy. They were living daily with the barbarity of animal packs, beginning to advance to the "law of talon" that limited retaliation to be allowed only relative to what was damaged or stolen. If you stole my daughter, I could only take one of your daughters, not kill your whole family. Inherent in these primitive laws was a step ahead of the savage status quo. You could not break all the teeth of a man who broke your tooth but only break one of his. The virtues of kindness and compassion seem to have been quietly brewing in kernel form even then.

Retaliation in public negotiations is visible in national politics today, and it remains a contributor to gridlock. Using such quietly brutal political tactics as stalling voting on confirmation of military offices or supreme court justices in the senate; refusing to bring for vote specific issues widely requested by the public such as gun control laws and tax regulation reform; and striving to defeat any bill proposed by the opposing party, easily remind one of the retaliative cultures of ancient Mesopotamia for which the Code of Hammurabi was designed. How slowly we evolve!

Justice as a virtue, at least in seminal form, remains crucial to be active in the character of every single political leader of today. Before we can count on a collaborative spirit in our leaders, there must at least be a genuine interest in fairness prodding each individual leader. How can a government address seriously such issues as systemic racism, gender inequality, burgeoning homelessness, and huge, even inhuman financial disparities if there is no real interest in basic fairness inside the hearts and minds of a majority of our top leaders?

While justice is the primary virtue dealt with in the Hammurabi Code, it is not the only one. A large percentage of the regulatory statements of the code pertain to efforts at maintaining enduring intimate loving relationships. Almost one-third of those primitive laws were about violence and other abuses at home, in domestic relationships that must have been quite painfully tumultuous.

For example:

[129]. If the wife of a man is taken in lying with another man, they shall bind them and throw them into the water. If the husband of the woman would save his wife, or if the king would save his male servant (he may).

[176]. And if a slave of the palace or a slave of the freeman takes the daughter of a man (gentleman); and if, when he takes her, she enter into the house of the slave of the palace or the slave of the freeman with the dowry of her father's house; if from the time that they join hands, they build a house and acquire property; and if later on the slave of the palace or the slave of the freeman die, the daughter of the man shall receive her dowry, and they shall divide into two parts whatever she and her husband had acquired from the time they joined hands; the owner of the slave shall receive one-half, and the daughter of the man shall receive one-half for her children.

The seeds of the virtue of chastity (Chapter 5, Chastity) were already gestating amidst the violent community chaos that unbridled animal sexual energy can generate. Their natural human sense that love is what we crave, not mere sex, was already sparking. It has come a long way today, but the too-frequent stories of love affairs seem to say we have a long way to go to understand the place of romance in the spiritual lives of politicians and most of us[vi] as well.

Assessing a candidate's character could well start with pointed questions about a candidate's possession and practice of that bedrock virtue, justice. This can be done, as will be shown later.

Moses et al. (14th-16th Centuries. BCE, Egypt, Jordan)

About 450 years later, another era in the evolution of virtue took place as centuries of oral tradition and discussions of what works in the developing of communal living finally came to be recorded among the ancient Hebrews. Estimated to have been about 1300 BC, some wisdom, probably generated by at least one group of older thinkers, influenced by similar deliberations in nearby cultures, emerged among those wandering people, and somebody eventually etched it down. Now called the Ten Commandments, they were attributed to Moses as ten imperative instructions as if the Divine Power (at times unnamed and for periods called YAHWEH) had commanded them (Exodus 20:2-17 and Deuteronomy 5: 6-21).

Those ten are still revered today by millions of Jews, Christians, and even secular entities who sense the great fledgling wisdom within those few words. Interpreted and re-interpreted innumerable times over the millennia by different faith groups, the Ten Commandments contribute to the evolving virtue language of seeking excellence among people. They seem designed by communications from YAHWEH to the Hebrew people, what kinds of behavior they would need to stop and what to learn in order to live in a genuine community, which had been already evolving orally by bits and inches for at least hundreds of years.

The values inherent in those commandments have lived and still influence societies to this day. They, too, apparently are designed as pragmatic. As "laws," they would serve to guide peoples' behavior, and when followed faithfully, they would help a community survive and even thrive. The last seven are more human than religious, except for the inference that they originated from the Divine. Indeed, they seem general and basic enough to apply usefully to any culture that would adopt them.

1. I am the Lord thy God. Thou shalt not have strange gods before me.

2. Thou shalt not take the name of the Lord, thy God, in vain.

3. Remember, make holy the Lord's Day.

4. Honor thy father and thy mother.

5. Thou shalt not kill.

6. Thou shalt not commit adultery.

7. Thou shalt not steal.

8. Thou shalt not bear false witness against thy neighbor.

9. Thou shalt not covet they neighbor's wife.

10. Thou shalt not covet thy neighbor's goods.

On close observation, these ten prohibitions indirectly teach and warn about how to ruin communal living and how to promote it with values and what we now can call hard-fought and acquired virtues. Seven of the ten (#4 to #10) are so basic and human that they continue to have high relevance for politics today. They are so general, however, that they have been argued about and even fought over much of the time since they were written in stone at the base of Mt. Sinai in Israel.

The introductory phrase of many of the ten is strong. *Thou shalt not* ... kill, steal, lie, or dishonor the magnificent natural phenomenon of intimate love. That wording leaves little room for discussion. Yet the commandments have resulted in millennia of controversy and splintering among people trying to understand, and both live by them and skirt around them. Is there such a thing as justified killing in a "just war" when the military of a bold and ruthless national leader attacks a small, peaceful neighbor and commences to kill and maim at will? Should an unrepentant suicidal mass murderer be allowed to keep living? Should we spend a large percent of our nation's funding on military weapons and "studying war" while still claiming to follow a prohibition "Thou shalt not kill."?

Early striving for virtuous living was probably rarely able to turn the tide of human weakness and already well-established self-indulgence. We as a human community began to learn what we are still learning – that virtue grows slowly with a series of events, decisions, and emotional/behavioral ingredients we continue trying to master. Rather than condemn those political candidates who have not yet found at least a minimum of some essential virtues, we'd best simply not invite them to serve in such vital capacities and seek to find those candidates who, to the closest look we can fathom, possess some semblance of those characteristics, and support their dedication to quality leadership for the good of global humanity.

Though the word virtue was not yet widely used, early Hebrews forcefully promoted the basics of human goodness in such virtues as honesty, justice, reverence for human life, care of parents (charity), chastity as honoring the romantic bond of lovers, as well as reverence for the Transcendent Power beyond us all. It is not difficult to see how some of these are still needed for the thriving of our own communities today.

- Lying in various forms is now threatening our communal trust.

- Pervasive greed is eroding our character.

- Sex without love, the antithesis of enduring romantic intimacy, continues to confuse us about such gnarly issues as transgender phenomena and abortion and contribute to the stealing of the deep satisfaction of our bonded relationships.

Isaiah (8th -7th centuries BCE, Judah, Israel)

Another high point in the evolution of virtue thinking and observation can be seen about six hundred years later, around 740-700 BC, in the same evolving Hebrew communities. Some teachers and priests of the ancient Hebrew tribes, perpetually yearning for decent leadership, were hoping for it in the form of a Messiah who would be, among other things, a magnificent leader. They pondered what he (we can bet they were sure it would be a man) would be like. In their deliberations, they imagined specific characteristics the Messiah would have when he would appear, a list found in the writings of the prophet Isaiah (Is 11:2-5). Previously character was mostly communicated by forbidding its opposites. This group had advanced to see, teach, and write about the positive characteristics of leaders they could mostly only dream about. Isaiah wrote:

The Spirit of the Lord will rest on him— the Spirit of wisdom and understanding, the Spirit of counsel and of might, the Spirit of the knowledge and fear of the LORD— and he will delight in the fear of the LORD. He will not judge by what he sees with his eyes or decide by what he hears with his ears; with righteousness he will judge people in need, with justice he will decide for the poor of the earth. He will strike the earth with the rod of his mouth; with the breath of his lips he will slay the wicked. Righteousness will be his belt and faithfulness the sash around his waist.

Eventually distilled from this listing of characteristics were what scholars came to call the Seven Gifts of the Holy Spirit (wisdom, understanding, knowledge, counsel, fortitude, piety, and "fear of the Lord") in Jewish and Christian teachings. Those seven characteristics came to be taught as virtues to be pursued by humans, though they are only rarely and episodically achieved to any great degree. They gave people targets for both their own movement towards contributing to communal richness and peace and for identifying leaders that would be better than average at governing. As humanity moves at a glacial pace towards a peaceful community, these seven serve as a roadmap for how people will need to function to facilitate that evolutionary movement. Politicians today could be facilitators of that persistent and generally messy development.

These named virtues offer a look into how Isaiah and those around him were thinking about the leadership they yearned for. They wanted in their top leader someone who had considerable *knowledge* about them and their day-to-day culture and problems; some *understanding* of their ways, struggles, and plight in life, and some willingness to get *counsel* about that from other thinkers, rather than deciding *for* them from a lofty, patronizing superiority. They visualized as ideal, a male dedicated to them, not merely to his own posh lifestyle. That is a functional definition of *piety* in government, a clear indication of political commitment to, and enthusiasm for, constituents and improving their day-to-day lives. He would have the *fortitude* (mighty) to stand *for* and *with* them among other nations and for standards of their behavior towards one another. And they would trust him more easily if he had some of the same *reverence* ("fear of the Lord"), a positive perspective on what is beyond us all, on which they relied.

Wisdom, a combination of all of this artfully put together, was, and still is, rare in leaders caught in the complexities of always needing to govern many diverse subjects at once, as well as recognizing and moderating their own thought-blurring self-interest. Wise politicians are still patently hard to find. But looking carefully for these seven positive characteristics can help us try and thereby further evolve.

Hebrew Compilations (c. 700 BC – 300 BC)

As leading Hebrews learned to write, what sounded good, accurate, and beautiful was compiled, first by oral repetition and then in scrolls and etchings. The Biblical book of Proverbs is a "compilation of compilations" that got attributed to Solomon due to his reputation as a wise leader but was no doubt written down by an unknown Hebrew thinker, or several of them. The last section of the book is an early description of a "virtuous woman" that alludes to many positive characteristics of women, probably written by a man. It is an early attempt to capture the characteristics of mature and admired women, especially thriving wives. The rather famous pericope is below in its entirety.

[10]. Who shall find a valiant woman? far and from the uttermost coasts is the price of her.

[11]. The heart of her husband trusteth in her, and he shall have no need of spoils.

[12]. She will render him good, and not evil all the days of her life.

[13]. She hath sought wool and flax, and hath wrought by the counsel of her hands.

[14]. She is like the merchant's ship, she bringeth her bread from afar.

[15]. And she hath risen in the night, and given a prey to her household, and victuals to her maidens.

[16]. She hath considered a field and bought it: with the fruit of her hands, she hath planted a vineyard.

[17]. She hath girded her loins with strength and hath strengthened her arm.

[18]. She hath tasted and seen that her traffic is good: her lamp shall not be put out in the night.

[19]. She hath put out her hand to strong things, and her fingers have taken hold of the spindle.

[20]. She hath opened her hand to the needy and stretched out her hands to the poor.

[21]. She shall not fear for her house in the cold of snow: for all her domestics are clothed with double garments.

[22]. She hath made for herself clothing of tapestry: fine linen and purple is her covering.

[23]. Her husband is honorable in the gates when he sitteth among the senators of the land.

[24]. She made fine linen and sold it, and delivered a girdle to the Canaanite.

[25]. Strength and beauty are her clothing, and she shall laugh in the latter day.

[26]. She hath opened her mouth to wisdom, and the law of clemency is on her tongue.

[27]. She hath looked well to the paths of her house and hath not eaten her bread idle.

[28]. Her children rose up and called her blessed: her husband, and he praised her.

[29]. Many daughters have gathered together riches: thou hast surpassed them all.

[30]. Favor is deceitful, and beauty is vain: the woman that feareth the Lord, she shall be praised.

[31]. Give her of the fruit of her hands: and let her works praise her in the gates. (Douay-Rheims American Edition)

It was one of the earliest and fullest attempts to capture the character traits of exceptional wives in specific and extrapolate to women in general. Highly idealistic, it nevertheless identifies several enduring and endearing qualities yearned for in a wife by men who were doing the writing. At least sixteen virtues are alluded to in that one section of Proverbs, including trustworthy, supportive, industrious, thrifty, domestically generous and skilled, physically sturdy, business savvy, charitable to the needy, ambitious, family dedicated, verbally wise and kind, socially confident, and reverently awed about the Beyond.

The writer acknowledges that beauty and charm are time-limited, and the virtuous woman far transcends that natural kind of obvious evaluation.

It is easy to see that every one of those admirable traits can apply to men as well and, as such, to every politician, male or female. While a politician is not necessarily a spouse, the domestic side of life and the arena of intimate loving carry rich parallels to a political career. The pursuit of people with a collaborative spirit for top political work can be informed by what it takes to be a quality-loving partner and parent. Most of those applicable traits are completely ignored in politics today. Such an adaptation of these characteristics to quality political success will also need to address the need, in both romance and politics, for persistent tolerance of one's partners' annoying imperfections, acceptance of their stubborn limitations, and considerable flexibility to "love-the-one-you're-with" dedication to the care for an intimate partner. (Cf. Chapter Five, Chastity).

Confucius (551 – 479 BC, Shandong, China)

There was an Asian component to the history of virtue too, as well as the Middle Eastern. Confucius (551-479 BC) was a teacher, philosopher, and champion of virtues, which he saw as the only way to effective government. He arose in China about 150 years after Isaiah wrote in what is now modern-day Iran.

Eventually, Confucius was widely referred to as the paragon of Chinese sages. But he died unsuccessfully. Through life experiences, he came to believe that helping youngsters learn about virtues early in life was the best way forward to a happy society. He spent much of his life trying to sell that idea and the content of his teaching, to the several kings around his home province to no avail. Then, a long time after his death, his teachings caught on and became the core of China's philosophical thinking and public education for centuries.

Confucius' basic teachings centered around cultivating oneself as a quality human being rather than learning a few concepts and following them or creating laws and keeping them.[vii] He taught a handful of virtues that formed the basis of his philosophy. But while he believed that those developed traits shaped people's childhood and then their adult relationships with one another and the state, he wasn't high on compliance to standards as much as catalyzing virtue within. He believed in teaching indirectly through examples, stories, and questions rather than direct memorizing and logical instruction.

Confucius's basic principles were called *ren, li, Yi, zhi,* and *xin*. They don't of course, translate exactly to western names for similar virtues. But all of them are relevant to political leadership today. Candidates stressing about getting elected could benefit from Confucius's advice: "Do not worry that you have no official position. Worry about not having the qualifications to deserve a position."

Confucius' key principles started with *ren*, what most people feel when they see a child hurting and in trouble. Ren is similar to the charity, compassion, or kindness of Judaism and Christianity, that at the time was yet to be widely spread. Translated most often as 'benevolence' or 'humanness', *ren* consisted of five basic virtues: seriousness, generosity, sincerity, diligence, and kindness.

All of these continue to stand as signposts for current politicians with issues involving children. Consider each of those five characteristics of *ren* regarding such issues as gun violence: *seriousness* (or solemnity) because there is no humor or goofiness when a child dies from a gun; *generosity* because the best motivation for fund raising is a children's hospital or hospice and children are only nurtured and raised through the generosity of adults; *sincerity* because what is phony, only silly, or sardonic screams out as obnoxious in the face of human pain. It is communication in depth with adults that children need most. And *diligence* because vivid human pain blares out responsibility for close and persistent attention, care, and responsive work right now.

For Confucius, augmenting *ren* was what he called *li*, a kind of ethics in three areas, paying attention to 1) ceremonies regarding ancestors, 2) social and political entities, and 3) daily etiquette. Those may sound archaic, but they speak to the formal responsibility for ritual a national leader carries when there is a significant major loss felt by most of the country's population, such as when a beloved leader dies or a natural disaster takes thousands of lives. Sensitivity to the need for national rituals and creativity for designing uniquely fitting ones are a component of building national pride as a plus for a top leader.

Reverence for meaningful ritual was a central reason there was so much outrage when a hoard of zealots swarmed into the U.S. national capital in January 2021 to stop a nearly sacred function of passing on presidential authority from one administration to another. While it is not the job of a national leader to design appropriate rituals for important occasions, it is their role to promote them and honor them with solemnity, reverence, and taste. Valuing that aspect of national leadership, however, while not a deal-breaker for choosing national leaders, remains a key value for quality leaders. Without it, at crucial times, there is only boorish groping that wastes tragic events that could consolidate camaraderie and communal support into an entire nation.

Paying attention to social and political entities as well as daily etiquette, can be seen as what we might call "class". Treating everyone around you with respect and honor becomes even more important for a top leader than its role for the rest of us. Not doing so should signal a lack of character that unnecessarily insults people, discourages them, internally angering and disgusting them and those who witness it. Slighting anyone publicly is far beneath the dignity of a top leader and can embarrass an entire nation on the international scene.

Yi is related to *li*. *Yi* is doing the right thing at the right time for the right reason, which is more for the good of others than for your own self-interest. Most everything a national political leader does in public affects their reputation and image. Some top leaders become used to almost automatically yet intentionally shaping their public behavior positively for its desired positive effect on their image to constituents, not necessarily for the good it does for the country. Eloquent words for those situations elude most of us at emotionally charged times. How do you keep the welfare of the people in your heart and mind by using words and policies that let people flow with their feelings and find meaning together?

Li is also the rare gift of being able to ignore self-interest, to think of what your people need and do your best to put your heart into it. In charged moments and days, self-interest as the primary motivator for public action comes through to many constituents as empty words or grandstanding. When such collusion between leader and followers becomes habitual, the credibility of the leader fades, at least among some subjects.

Close to the western concept of wisdom was a fourth principle, *zhi*, the art of using knowledge to make good decisions for oneself and others. We can see here a strong parallel to the knowledge-understanding-wisdom trilogy of Isaiah. (See above, Chapter Two, Isaiah, and Chapter Four, Savvy). Great minds sometimes find similar themes evolving in pondering what is best for humanity.

Finally, Confucius taught about *xin*, usually translated as fidelity, meaning a natural cognitive-emotional knowing and attachment to people and specific ideas—a kind of interpersonal, communal savvy. "Who does a candidate quote as inspiring examples" in lectures and campaign speeches, and "What is the sense of those quotes?" Hearing a candidate talk seriously about their *xin* and answering probing questions about it can be quite revealing about that person's character. Asking a candidate in public what they treasure, what they would die for, what is their highest value, and carefully watching their facial expression as they respond will show an indication of the presence of *xin* in that candidate.

Our national leaders could well further cultivate their *xin* about all of humanity, keeping the various world peoples in their hearts as well as on their minds. We assume they have a measure of *ren*, but some don't seem to, when their meanness or blind neglect of diverse populations can be astounding. A greater degree of *yi* would counter the rather obvious self-interest preoccupation and the raw thirst for power that show through some leaders' public behaviors.

Confucius saw virtuous *actions* tied to cultivating *knowledge*, one augmenting the other, a perennial struggle, almost an open debate at times, in religion. (Is it what you believe or what you do that matters most? Your faith or your loving action?) In each candidate, we can ask ourselves, in encountering them, are their thinking and education overshadowing and thus destructive to their heartfelt fidelity, reverence, and commitment to high standards? Or is cognition a guide for them in meeting the always confusing issues of justice and truth that ought not be reduced to dualistic over-simplification? To Confucius, more a philosopher than a theologian, a virtuous disposition could make you naïve to exploitation, and virtuous action without knowledge the mere compliance to a guru or cult leader, like an automaton. Exploring the degree of integration of the two, positive action and positive knowledge, will be difficult. However, engaging a candidate about that integration contributes to the career shaping of that future leader.

How far should faithful allegiance to the *xin* of a political party go in determining the decision-making of a congressperson? Where is conscience and critical thinking of one's own in risking momentous decisions for the good of the people? Wisdom, indeed, is almost always elusive in crucial matters.

Plato (c. 427-c. 347 BC, Athens) and the Hellenists

About the same time as Confucius was striving to raise standards of virtuous humanness in China, the *classic Greeks* in Athens, in what has been called the very first graduate school, were philosophizing directly about the virtues of what they were calling an "ethical leader of an ethical society." Plato and his mentor, Socrates, and his students, including Aristotle (fifth and fourth centuries BC), made lasting contributions to the slowly growing body of virtue lore emerging from dialogues about Greek politics of the times.

The Hellenists defined and described a distillation of four virtues observed to be needed by any leader of a healthy or ethical society: *prudence, justice, temperance, and fortitude.* These basic characteristics were picked up by early Christian writers a half millennium later and then amplified by medieval Catholic theologians as cardinal or pivotal virtues for any spiritual life. All four of these core virtues stand as relevant attributes for the character of our national leaders. Ourselves as well, of course, but leaders stand out as bold examples for us all – in one direction or the other.

The Greeks' development of virtue concepts was pragmatic more than religious and ascetic as well as functional. Hippocrates, a partial contemporary and forerunner of Plato, had already separated science from religion, and the Hellenists were certainly on the science side of that division. They were philosophers, having learned to prescind from religious and other spiritual systems they saw as less likely to stand up to critical thinking and open human debate. They saw that government simply does not work, especially for the common person, without a measure of these four virtues in the top leaders.

Justice - Citizens always have an eye out for justice, with a keen sense of when they are being treated unfairly, especially by top leadership. In The Republic, Plato is said to have noted that "Without leaders with some sensitivity to *fairness,* the people will suffer." That seems to be what motivated Hammurabi's code, too. Both men hated how people were continually hurt by one another's mistreatment, though we are now aware of how, in practice, this consideration did not always extend equally to women, culturally different people, and even all men.

While law isn't necessary for the few good people who have a sense of fairness built into them or established by previous experience, the law is still needed to recognize and categorize unfairness among people. It is natural for individuals at this stage of evolution to be somewhat self-centered, just as it is somewhat natural for us to be episodically considerate and kind. An internal sense of justice remains today one piece of the pedestal on which true leaders stand. While knowing that pervasive justice is still a target, not a given, vying for it remains a major component of the collaborative spirit we voters need to examine in candidates.

Temperance– *A disciplined sense of needing moderation of one's natural tendencies towards excess* is what allows a person to find objectivity amidst the human proclivity for such impulses as overeating, drunkenness, loveless sex, greed, and anger at not getting our way. The excesses of leaders who lack *temperance* will make them destructive with their drinking, self-indulgent partying, laziness, or boorish neglect of responsibility to do anything useful. The "town drunk" has been around as long as people have distilled fruit juice, representing a wasted life, eventually losing or destroying every relationship with anyone who once cared about them. Alcoholism was not discovered to be a treatable illness until as recently as the early-twentieth century. The impression of excessive anger, impulsiveness, narrowness, secretiveness, and occasional blind acquiescence to others are clues to a candidate's need to further develop sobriety and character before taking top leadership positions.

Fortitude - In their academic explorations and debates about political leader qualities, the Hellenists came to see that courage combined with focused strength was indispensable in a top leader, too. Without a considerable measure of this combination called *fortitude,* which stands against the destructive forces of nature and harmful human behavior, top leaders will give way to threatening influences — both domestic political party churning and foreign military upheavals. In prehistory, recounting events of courageous heroes made some of the best fireside story telling. Strength and courage were highly valued even in the animal world, a likely reason that weaker pack members – the old, injured, undernourished, and sick – were undervalued in that might-makes-right phase of evolution.

Prudence - Without the discretion of *prudence,* top leaders will make fools of themselves in most every public appearance, losing the respect of both subjects and adversaries and never even approaching wisdom on anything important except by coincidence. Prudence is a moment of awareness of how a spoken thought or action will uniquely fit a given situation before implementing it, or not. A situational form of wisdom, prudence includes patience to quickly reflect on how to meet specific, often unpredictable events with savvy, restraint, and brief, momentary forethought. In electoral selections, lack of it warns of who and what to avoid and can point to impulsive participation in what may trouble followers' confidence about a candidate's ability to lead with good sense.

As Medieval Catholic theologians were pondering the notion of virtue, at least one of them, Thomas Aquinas, picked up these four key qualities, and in discussions, they eventually became the Cardinal Virtues of traditional Catholic teaching. (Cardinal from Latin, *cardo*, *cardinalis* meaning, pertaining to a hinge, that on which something turns or depends.) A great deal now hinges on top leaders demonstrating significant levels of these four characteristics.

One general observation Plato and his followers made was honoring the limitation of regulation's ability to establish peace and prosperity. Law, beginning around Hammurabi's time, has brought a speck of predictability to the world, as evidenced by such standards as traffic rules that have brought order to driving and transportation in general. But situational drama still pervades much of life, and prudence is what takes it seriously and avoids either exacerbating it or being embarrassed by it. Effective prudence requires quick thoughtfulness, which is strangely common in people with deep character. "Good people do not need laws to tell them to act responsibly, while bad people will find a way around the laws." (Plato, <u>Philosopher Kings</u>)

Jesus of Nazareth (c. ~4 BC - 33 AD)

As the primary figure of Christianity, Jesus of Nazareth was a most remarkable virtue contributor. Though he never wrote anything that has yet been found, he made dozens of statements publicly that were recorded by the Biblical writers Mark, Matthew, and others, that seem to have changed millions of peoples' hearts over the past twenty-two centuries. His unique focus on the value of interpersonal care, the profound value of every person, the centrality of human charity, fierce loyalty to "the good," stark honesty about injustice, endurance rather than retaliation, and widespread forgiveness for all past regretted actions — set the stage for a religious movement that spread rapidly across the known western world after his death.

Born a Jew and educated as a rabbi, Jesus was a carpenter turned itinerant preacher, executed for causing political upheaval. His words, written down by evangelists Mark, Mathew, Luke, John, and others, presented a radical new way to live, free of many of the burdensome beliefs and regulations that hung on peoples' dispositions in their day-to-day lives. An example of his radical teaching is illustrated by a single story, not to be taken literally, about what happens after death and what that means to how we live. It is now found in the New Testament of the Bible, Matthew 25: 31-40. The story is set in the scene of the afterlife when deceased people are forming two lines in front of "The King," sheep to his right and goats to his left. The story continues:

> [34]"Then the King will say to those on his right, `Come, you who are blessed by my Father; take your inheritance, the kingdom prepared for you since the creation of the world.

> [35] For I was hungry, and you gave me something to eat; I was thirsty, and you gave me something to drink; I was a stranger and you invited me in; 36 I needed clothes, and you clothed me; I was sick, and you looked after me; I was in prison, and you came to visit me." (Matt 25)

In turn, he says the reverse to the goats, sending them to eternal fire for ignoring the hungry, the thirsty, the strangers, the sick, the naked, and the imprisoned.

He concludes the story with verse 40: "Whatever you did for the least of your brethren [sic], you did to me".

In that story, Jesus is presented as teaching that the only thing genuinely important in life is how you treat those in dire need. Charity for needy people is what counts most—a tough teaching indeed.

Around that notion, Jesus' followers built the original foundation of Christianity as actively caring about other people, especially the disadvantaged. That aspect of one's life must be added to the list of virtues needed by political leaders. A candidate's history of charity is at least a bit revealing about them and their character. It is doubtful if a list of causes to which one has contributed financially is what is meant by charity in the story. These actions of facing the needy and caring for any of them directly, personally, and generously – the hungry, the bereft, the ragged – tell something intimate about a person and their character that is essential to being a fine leader. (See Chapter 4, Kindness in the Moment) Conversely, a candidate who can ignore that segment of society that can never seem to get started at fashioning a useful and enjoyable life does not qualify to be a leader of humanity or even a country, city, or town. While the unsheltered wanderer not only remains with us, seemingly in perpetuity, ignoring them as a political leader signals a kind of "ignore-ance" that perpetuates such errant phenomena as a *kleptocracy* and constitutes a missing piece in the personality of that top leader.

Saul of Tarsus (Paul the Apostle) (c. 5 – c. 65 AD Turkey - Rome)

Early Christians, as recorded by Paul of Tarsus (St. Paul, to Christians), contributed heavily and broadly to the development of positive character language. Paul was the most prolific spreader of the new emotionally enlivening community of early Christianity, and he was the clearest articulator of the values and highly appealing teachings of Jesus, though the two of them apparently never met in person. As the probable writer of Galatians (Gal 5: 22-23), for example, Paul noticed stark differences in the people who converted to the energetic and enthusiastically loving new Christian communities and those who did not convert. As described by Paul, the new groups of followers of Jesus were a happy lot, compelling as neighbors and astoundingly resilient as martyrs. They were seen exhibiting a cluster of virtues, eventually called the Fruits of the Spirit (charity, joy, peace, patience, benignity, gentleness, trustfulness, hopefulness, and "longsuffering" (resilience.)[viii]

This breakthrough to highly positive and compelling traits effectively transformed thousands of people across the Mediterranean as the original Christian movement. Catholic schools of the twentieth-century U.S. did a far better job of teaching us how to recite those characteristics than about how to live them. They tried. (I was eventually one of those teachers for a time. I'd give myself a D+.) It is easier to focus language on negative words – psychopathology, sin, vice, mental illnesses, and crass epithets – than expand the use of positive personal traits. The internet has not yet improved this.

Paul saw that those who did not convert were more likely to be people who exhibited negative behaviors, such as, "sexual immorality, impurity and debauchery; idolatry and witchcraft; hatred, discord, jealousy, fits of rage, selfish ambition, dissensions, factions and envy; drunkenness, orgies, and the like." (Galatians 5: 19-21). These negative characteristics and actions eventually became known as the *seven deadly sins* in Medieval times. They can be seen as the antithesis of virtues and applicable to most of us at times, including some national leader behavior.

The brief descriptions of the enthusiasm, kindness, and joy of early Christian communities eventually became adopted into Catholic catechisms and other Christian education materials as the Fruits of the Spirit. Several of these were new additions to the previously named virtues, and some reiterated positive characteristics that had been named earlier in history.

The remarkable *joy* of early Christians for example, was phenomenal and became legendary, even recorded as persisting during persecution all the way to martyrdom. Patience and the generosity of chastity, which become essential in secondary stages of intimate loving[viii], are clearly named here. These are observable in a few national legislators, even in the midst of their conflict-filled daily relationships. They just seem mostly happy, highly tolerant, and settled. The U.S. needs more leaders like that.

Francis of Assisi (1181-1226 AD, Italy) and the Evangelical Counsels

Francis of Assisi was the only chief figure of the Protestant Reformation who did not leave the Catholic Church. Agreeing that the Church leaders had fallen into horrible degeneration, he sought to improve the Church by inner life focus, lifestyle example, humanistic generosity, good-hearted teaching, and establishing a religious order in which men, and later women, could dedicate their work lives to the poor and cultivate one another's human spirits in the process. How Francis's order contributed to the evolution of virtue can be summarized in the three vows taken by members at some point in their development, generally in the presence of a community that is still called the three *evangelical counsels*.

Religious orders of men and women, mostly Roman Catholic, comprise a significant offshoot development of Christian culture. These were groups of men, and eventually, groups of women too, who did not marry and dedicated themselves to community life and to caring for the poor, sick, and marginalized. About a hundred years after this movement of religious orders began, Francis, in the early part of the thirteenth century, renewed them. He wrote about how his followers should live together in some semblance of peace and cooperation, centered on care for the poor. As part of this philosophy, the evangelical counsels were based on "Evangelical," meaning "of the gospel". The members focused their lives on three virtues that made them distinct from other contemporary Christians: *poverty, chastity,* and *obedience.* All three have relevance for political leaders as they are also committed, at least formally, to working together for the country and its constitution.

While politicians are not expected to pursue personal perfection, a pragmatic interpretation of these vows makes them relevant for exploring a candidate character.

The vow of *poverty,* for example, has relevance for developing a degree of communal thrift (Chapter Four, Thrift) in applicants for national political office. For monks, that vow was radical. They agreed, indeed vowed, to own almost nothing, being given what they needed day to day by an abbot or prefect who was replaced by another monk elected every few years. It allowed order members to concentrate on charitable works rather than on supporting themselves financially and a family. Sharing together all they earn and gather from contributions, they vowed never to possess much money. They were supported financially by the community resources, and they contributed to those resources by what they earned through work they did and donations they received. That reduced the natural human pressure to always better themselves financially and materially, which in excess results in destructively wasteful greed.

Put simply, members of religious orders theoretically never have to worry about money because they won't have any except what they need, and that much will always be there. They lived simply and were remunerated equally to one another, reducing envy and greed. They were, and are, a lot who are quite dedicated to humanity and to spiritual life. Women religious established, for example, most of the non-state hospitals in the United States. All of this is despite the spiritual erosion that takes place in some members who fail to keep those vows. That lifestyle turned out to be not appropriate or even possible for most people.

The vow of *obedience* simplified their decisions about their work venues, where to live, and particularly, who to listen to in the face of big decisions. (Latin *obediens* - listening). Having already decided to permanently surrender major aspects of their life decision power to the current head of the community, they tended to get more work done without wrangling with leadership, already established community values, and keeping order in petty conflicts among them. While today's politicians may not need a vow of obedience, they sure could take a lesson from this evangelical council to listen carefully rather than so continually seek to teach, influence, and even intimidate one another and sometimes the people as well.

The vow of *chastity* was an agreement to abstain from sex if single and be faithful to one partner if they were married. Generally, they were not married. That freed them from managing the complexities and vagaries of a romantic love life – they agree to have no sexual relationships, so they were (and still are) freer to give their days to care for the poor, work for charity, create hospitals, establish schools, teach at every level, and develop quality, sustaining, and creative friendships. The clergy sex abuse scandals since 2001 have drastically tarnished respect for this virtue in many eyes. But the virtue itself, the integrity of how one copes with and enjoys the uncontrollable itches of sexual energy with a perpetual vigilance for the effect it has on other people and even oneself, remains ideal for politicians as well as everybody else. (See Chastity, Chapter 4)

For today's politicians, there is wisdom in the evangelical counsels accurately interpreted. They are not related to today's evangelical Christians, a cross-denominational set of strongly held basic beliefs. The evangelical counsels of Francis suggest that you avoid preoccupations with greed and sexual impropriety and decide carefully who you follow and how stringently. Reduce distractions of excess when you are elected to public office and contribute as much as you can of your freedom, care, and life energy to the people you serve. Dedication to the good of humanity remains much needed by political leaders. (See Benignity and Dedication to Humanity, Chapter 3)

One other Medieval writer, Abbot Bernard of Clairvaux, made two additions to this brief virtue history. One of them is his eighty sermons on the spirituality of romantic love, seeing the relationship between lovers as a reflection of the love between people and God. The other is his cluster of convictions and writing about humility[xi]. He wrote and taught as intensely as anyone else about the virtue of humility. Phrases for which he is known include "without humility, there is no spirituality" and "the three most important virtues are humility, humility, and humility." He saw that the capacity to realistically appraise yourself among God and other people is so basic that nothing else mattered if you didn't possess at least a bit of humility to counter pride on one hand and self-denigration or false pride on the other.

Other Medieval Catholic Theologians

Catholic theologians in Medieval times exhibited two characteristics that make their contributions to virtue development valuable. First, they would adopt previously established concepts, like Plato's four essential virtues that made good philosophical and human sense, and incorporate them into traditional Catholic teaching. And second, they were motivated to promote healthy living the best they knew how using the Christian history they loved to promote to that end. Thus, the virtues named in traditional Catholic spiritual theology are, in essence, sometimes almost identical with the meanings of earlier virtue teachers like Plato, Confucius, and especially the ancient Hebrew writers.

In terms of virtue evolution, the Reformation's famous Catholic-Protestant skirmishes included a de-emphasis in Protestant movements on teaching virtues. The Protestant reformers were busy championing mostly faith as a gift of God. They sometimes reduced it to the only necessary element for salvation. The Catholic practice of focusing on virtue thinking and practice was perceived by them as bringing back people's reliance on their own behavior for being ready for paradise after death, an element of Catholic belief they disdained. There seemed to be no clear place for that soteriology in Protestant thinking. Even forty years ago, and to some degree today, virtue language is most often seen as Catholic and mostly foreign sounding and suspicious or naive and idealistic to Protestants and uninvolved people on the street. Yet virtues have been closer to humanistic references to solid character than to religious purity. As such, they could become beacons to help to guide us and our leaders on the stormy seas of politics today and tomorrow.

Benjamin Franklin (1706-1790)

Called one of the world's most successful men, Franklin has the distinction of having devised for himself in his youth a list of virtues to which he would aspire in his life. He commented near his death that though he hadn't attained the virtuous aspirations he'd hoped for, he believed that he was a better man over his lifetime because he had intentionally decided on pursuing them as a young man. He clearly knew early in his life what virtue was and adopted some names of virtues from history. His list for his own growth and development included temperance, silence, resolution, order, frugality, industry, sincerity, prudence, justice, moderation, cleanliness, tranquility, chastity, and humility.

His selections indicate his exceptional reflection on himself and on humanity. To other historical lists of virtues, he added *silence*, a monastic teaching to open and calm oneself for the emergence of the new *resolution*, by which he seems to have meant only speak what will help yourself or somebody else; *order*, the settling of one's anxiety by seeking precision in how your material possessions are consistently patterned; *industry* or industriousness, a developed trait of getting things done, against the natural human penchants for laziness and seeking of comfort; *sincerity*, the capacity to find solemnity and soul amidst the superficiality of social and political engagement; and *cleanliness*, maintaining a bodily freshness and personal simplicity, for one's own good and those around.

All these presumably would make one's life clearer, more comfortably directed, relaxing, and productive. As the only person on this list of historical virtue influencers who indeed was a political leader, Franklin stands as a bright light for other politicians regarding how he cultivated himself by intentionally growing virtue in himself to make him a better leader of people. And was then graceful with himself for not perfectly having achieved much of that in his lifetime. He can easily be seen as a clear example of "missing the mark" of his original virtue ambitions and forgiving himself for even quite striking transgressions and omissions, apparently rather easily.

Pierre Teilhard de Chardin, S.J. (1881 – 1955)

In his thinking and writing, Pierre Teilhard de Chardin saw love of all kinds and dimensions as central, not only to humanity but to the evolution of the universe itself. An accomplished though mediocre paleontologist, Jesuit priest, evolutionary philosopher, and creative theologian, he is best remembered as a mystic and visionary of the path of evolution and its probable next endpoint, a global loving community. He celebrated the energy that holds the atom's nucleus together, draws atoms into molecules, joins molecules into cells, cells into organs, and people to one another into community, as all the same entity. Now that we have evolved into beings who can think, love, and decide, we can influence the path of evolution itself towards its apparent next stage, the "omega point", a global community of loving people waiting for the next phase whatever it might be. The frontier of that evolutionary process is small groups of individuals engaging with authenticity to improve the care of people. (See Chapter 6, CPE)

Pierre Teilhard's thinking continues: Once life appeared at a few places on the planet, there began the formation of a *biosphere,* a layer of life that continued to expand and deepen until it now encompasses the earth and continues to grow. Then, when consciousness emerged in the evolutionary process, it began a *noosphere,* a layer of thought that gradually encircled the planet and continues today in all that is known, thought, and cognitively developed in people's minds, as evident in books, think tanks, universities, and the internet and now artificial intelligence. And beyond those two, the biosphere and the noosphere, there is a third layer forming, one of human care, empathy, charity, and love of all kinds. He called it an *amortisphere,* a love sphere of acting kindly, supportively, and sometimes carefully challenging one another beyond animal affinities. It is all progressing haltingly and ever so gradually towards some unimagined global loving community. Every positive comment, genuine smile, helping gesture, affectionate kiss, gentle embrace, tender caress, loving carnal embrace, and warm, friendly greeting moves that process along just a bit and contributes to the very process of universal evolution.

Teilhard can be included in this overview of virtue history because he built his philosophy on the human characteristic of care, already enshrined by the ancient Jews[xii], Jesus, Paul of Tarsus, and Christianity in general, as the central characteristic in the makeup of persons. As a mystical clinician of sorts, Teilhard would have us to discern the presence of showing kindness in the moment as a necessary characteristic of all top political leader candidates. Can the voter see and feel a loving heart in this political candidate? (See "Kindness in the Moment," discussed in Chapter Four).

Carol Gilligan (1936—XXXX)

As women gradually found their voices among the more strong-in-the-shoulders men, mostly in the past century, they have contributed to virtue conceptualizing more by example than by writing. To begin with, the notion of "a virtuous woman" has been de-emphasized as meaning only being compliant to what men want or being overly careful at indulging and exploiting it. The movement in recent decades seems to have featured women finding their voice, their own mind, and indeed, finding themselves, taking their place, and shaping their own lives. Jeanne d'Arc, known as Joan of Arc (1412-1431), had been a precursor of that.

Jeanne d'Arc doesn't seem to have written anything that lasted, but she stands as shining an example of courage and conviction as anyone in history. Having been burned at the stake at age 19 for alleged demon possession and for impersonating a man to become a soldier at 17, she left behind admirable military accomplishments and became a patron saint of France. While some historians gingerly question her mental health, she is also called an early feminist, and her image is found in art all over the world.

A list of great women would be long, from the very early Hebrew prophetess Deborah, the Medieval counselor of kings, Catherine of Sienna, to Angela Merkel, Madame Curie, Margaret Thatcher, Amelia Earhart, and the recently deceased Queen Elizabeth. But in terms of virtue language in general, Carol Gilligan should appropriately be mentioned as well.

A Harvard developmental psychologist, Gilligan expressed her creative ideas primarily in her classes and in a seminal book entitled In a Different Voice: Psychological Theory and Women's Development (Harvard University Press: 1982). It is significant here because she taught from her research that women's path through human development differs greatly from that of men, who had been the subjects of most all developmental theorists of history, including such famous ones as Freud, Erikson, Piaget, and Kohlberg. The following interpretation is that of this author.

Gilligan saw women as more highly valuing *relationships* than *autonomy* as they were growing up, the opposite of men's development as seen in the established theories. That made *trust* a bigger issue for women since a close relationship requires more vulnerability than seeking autonomy does. In terms of virtue language, women seem to naturally use vulnerability to retain ties to people even as men were persistently moving towards dominance and greater personal confidence and freedom for themselves. Despite women's traditionally weaker physical strength and the sexual vulnerability of potential pregnancy, they highlight a need to use vulnerability to move forward in development through relationships. That points to another virtue that helps people succeed in political negotiations. *Interpersonal faith,* or *trust in the goodness of the other.* That as a political asset is mostly missing in modern-day U.S. politics.

The term *trustfulness* is mentioned (in some translations), or faithfulness, as a virtue by Paul of Tarsus in the list of the Fruits of the Spirit (Gal 5: 21-22) but it is not described, nor even defined. It is not only trust, though, but trust-FULL-ness. Paul apparently saw easy trust experientially in new Christian converts, and it was striking to him. Apparently, trust was not common among people at that time in history, as it certainly is not today, especially in politics. Fear was probably at least as prevalent in people then as anxiety and depression are now. In fact, what could be seen as the opposite of trustfulness, i.e., suspicion, is more prevalent in national politics than any confidence in colleagues, let alone in political adversaries. Trusting other politicians, especially those of a different party, is seen as folly, naivete, gullibility, or a major weakness. Carol Gilligan and others like Brene Brown may have brought it back, but it remains fledgling.

Though several other women's developmental experts criticized the Gilligan research and theory, that book still guided many women to find their own voices while gingerly dodging the heavy paternalistic culture of the time that persists today. Now, forty years later, Gilligan was about to publish In a Human Voice, hopefully to assert that the use of one's vulnerability is necessary for intimacy and close, treasured relationships for both men and women, including in same-sex relationships. The advice, "warm up!" in all kinds of relationships, could be useful to many constituents as well as their politicians if we could deeply hear it.

Seligman and Positive Psychology

When Martin Seligman was elected president of the American Psychology Association in 1998, he chose *positive psychology* as the theme of his term. Thus, it was newly energized a move[xii] to counter the pervasive tone of psychology as focusing on the negative – maladaptive behavior, mental illness, and disordered personalities. Positive psychology is a growing field of human development, partly because it makes sense. If psychology is to be the "study of the mind," then virtue is a logical sub-specialty. Some psychology practitioners had grown weary of the over-focus on the negative perspectives of psychopathology. They began to develop studies and conceptual views of people's positive traits and happiness, seeking functional ways of assisting the evolution of the human species.

There is still a great need to focus on what is wrong with troubled and troubling people with scientific objectivity and research. Regarding national leaders, both negative and positive views are needed in pondering their character. There are those top leaders who probably need professional assistance, those who could benefit from guided personal growth, and those who ought not to be leading millions of people at all. And there are those who should be more highly appreciated for their healthy practicality, positive purpose, and virtue. Sorting out which group a given candidate belongs to best can be a partnership between assessors of character and psychological diagnosticians.

Since Seligman's re-energizing of the evolution of virtue as useful and even vital to human wellness and collaborative community, the assessment of character through research on virtue as related to personal and communal happiness has continued to grow as a domain in psychology. It rebirths what the classic Greeks called the pursuit of *eudaimonia*, "the good life."

A comprehensive example of seeing virtues and positive character traits as a valuable perspective is Seligman's own tome (with Christopher Peterson). Character Strengths and Virtues: A Handbook and Classification[xiii], (2004). It describes hundreds of studies that attempt to get a handle on the positive characteristics that contribute to "the good life."

Research itself, though, has its limitations in advancing the understanding and enjoyable living of real people. In personal and interpersonal matters, research does have its benefits in insight and understanding, to a degree. But in some minds, it can easily become a substitute for actually relating interpersonally and continually improving how to do that. Insight has a way of making you feel like you have really learned something, though you haven't changed your behavior at all. Unless you can use research practically, it contributes only academically to society. The neo-empiricism popular in many fields today will likely subside, almost as if it were another fad. Research will, no doubt, always provide some solid data and conceptualizing to give direction to the helping professions. It will first need, however, to get over its preoccupation with chasing impossible certitude to take its proper place in the evolution of virtue in society.

*   *   *   *

The implication in all these teachings, and many others throughout history, such as the Hindu, Taoist, and hundreds of native culture words, is that we humans need to consider virtues as targets to be aimed at in all our affairs. That is not old-fashioned. It is the way of the future. Maybe it's the only way. The world needs a character view of leadership. One piece of that examination path is recognizing and assessing the virtues of applicants for national political office.

Chapter Three:

Nine Essentials of a Collaborative Spirit

Character assessment involves looking at a person from several perspectives. It is not a dualistic process easily lending itself to answers of yes or no. Perspective (etymologically, looking at something through something else) differs based on the place from which you are viewing. But it also differs based on the lens of the device through which it is being viewed. Below is a set of lenses from which each of us can view a given candidate. How we will see that person will of course, depend on our own points of view, such as our individual preferences, personal history, conscious and unconscious biases, and solidly shaped political attitudes. At the least, these virtue category lenses provide a language in which to consider and discuss the depth and color of human character. The central question to carry in an assessment is, "Does this candidate exhibit any indicators of possessing at least a vestige of the essential virtues?"

The following nine virtues are chosen intuitively as directly related to collaboration, an essential component of flourishing political leadership. They may well be researched eventually for more data indicating validity and reliability. However, creative conceptualization and inspiring perspectives precede research. Such highly successful new socio-psycho-spiritual entities as Alcoholics Anonymous, Clinical Pastoral Education, and group psychotherapy began and proceeded to develop without research or even philosophical sophistication to lead their way. They emerged from dire need coupled with new adaptations of established conceptual frameworks, unpredictable inspiration, and shared dedicated collaborative work as they developed pragmatic practices to relieve intense human predicaments and suffering. The following elements of a plan for assessing character may follow that pattern as well, leaving research for later after accumulation of data availability[xiv].

In this next chapter, many suggestions are presented that will make better sense after reading Chapter Five about the three methods of assessing character – (direct individual observation, large group engagement, and small group confrontation.) That is especially true about the challenging questions suggested for eliciting further disclosures by candidates about their underlying character. Some readers may choose to read Chapter Five before this one.

1. Justice – A Habitual Sense of Fairness

Even on the playground, few youngsters want to play with the kid who cheats. In Congress, however, it depends on who is cheating and how. Can you collaborate with someone who does not have embedded within them a reasonable sense of fairness? Apparently so. But at what cost?

The traditional pledge of allegiance to the flag of the United States of America ends with the words "...with liberty and justice for all". Justice is artistically depicted as a blindfolded woman holding up a scale for balancing weights on each side, presumably to bring them to fair equality. But the truth in any age about justice may be closer to the 1979 Al Pacino movie (directed by Norman Jewison) "With Liberty and Justice for All." It was one of the first films to impress on viewers the complexity of the U.S. justice system and how unlikely it is to find consistent justice there. That is the pervasive situation of human society so far.

For a speck of hope, we'd best believe that justice is evolving among us. Advertisements, tweets, and even news reports certainly don't make it look like that! A viable choice is to believe that we are collectively not getting worse with one another. It is simply hard to accept that the evolutionary process is so slow, though accelerated by the arrival of evolving human beings with the capacity to think and to choose. Comparing the subjects of Hammurabi to the automobile traffic regulations of today's cities certainly seems to show progress. Even villains mostly keep traffic laws. And bend to penalties when they are caught.

Scholars have long distinguished four types of justice that determine how injustice is pursued by societies. They are distributive justice (a fair division of material worth), subsidiary justice (fair treatment of organizational inferiors), retributive justice (fair punishment for wrongdoing), and restorative justice (efforts to apply healing action to wrongdoing)[xv].

An example of *distributive* justice would be how an observer (candidate) feels when watching a video of a slender, minimally educated man quivering as he subjects himself to an armed tax collector, hoping to Allah the man will not take from him his one sheep or three chickens needed to feed his three children this week. Does the candidate feel that internal ache for the man's situation, the likes of which are common in some parts of the world? That hurt is indeed a personal sign of the virtue of distributive justice. He will be likely to carry it with him in determinations of wealth inequality if elected. There is no telling what he will do with it then, however. One example that will manifest retributive justice in a candidate would be how that candidate feels inside their gut watching a young man gazing wistfully between bars of a prison, having had 15 years of his freedom taken away for a third minor drug selling infraction at the age of sixteen, perhaps a substance that is now legal in 22 states. Seizing an individual's freedom and ability to shape their own life is a horrible act. What is needed in a case to make it just? For our purposes here, we are more interested in justice as a virtue in a person than in philosophical or practical thinking about how to deal with injustice in a community. A contemporary Jewish Rabbi wrote:

But for a society to operate with full justice we need righteous humans. For peace and justice to prevail in society, we do not require only laws of justice, but also people of justice. That is to say, justice as a virtue of political institution should be brought in relation to justice as a virtue of character. Dr. Yasien Mohamed [xvi]

As a virtue in a candidate, for example, justice can be seen as a jab in their heart or stomach when they observe stark unfairness or even hear stories of somebody boldly and brutally being treated wrongly. Observing the early development of my only granddaughter made me believe that the organic mechanism of a sense of justice grew as part of our character when we were small and everybody with overt power was big. Justice was a keen little internal observer, and we quickly felt hurt when wronged by a probing or aggressive adult or an insensitive peer. As an individual toddler, you may have been feisty and oppositional about being left out, pushed around, or treated roughly. Or the feeling of injustice may have run silently in you, waiting, hoping for better days to find words, begin to hazard protesting, and then engage in it vociferously when it felt safe enough. We all eventually find out that life itself is very unfair in many ways and constantly so. But a sense of justice is still perceptible if you listen carefully to that faint pain in your heart at witnessing serious injustice. Conscience is a similar voice regarding our own behavior as it sees ourselves acting unjustly towards others or a community. Justice as a virtue is often partially visible upon addressing it.

One vital motivating factor for collaboration is a piercing internal sense of abhorrence for injustice. We, voters, should favor leaders who have such a resilient sense of unfairness almost anywhere they look. Not that even top leaders can do much about increasing justice in many issues of a relatively young evolutionary world that is only a few millennia from settling issues with fangs and claws. But allowing the heart to feel the pain of others treated badly, even when there is no good and realistic way to make some situations better, keeps that heart ready to do what it can when opportunities do arise. Then, a collaborative spirit can motivate to act.

How can voters confront a political candidate about their sense of justice? One way would be to give a bold description of the life and current story of one of those long-time unsheltered wanderers, here or abroad, and observe the candidate's response. What emotions does it seem to generate in that candidate, if any? Do they even see a justice issue here, or only blame somebody else and claim to be feeling sympathy? How hidden are their feelings? Is there no sign of a lively internal struggle regarding the life plight apparent in people barely coping with an unjust world, the unsheltered wanderers that range in droves in some cities? Is there a part of that candidate that grapples with the empathy, sadness, hurt, and frustration in themselves that runs parallel to the chronic feelings of those wanderers? Follow-up questions could ask about this candidate's previous efforts to address, cope with, and accept the massive injustice involved in some unfair aspects of the modern economy and, thus, unfortunately, wasted lives.

The intent here is not to expect a justice activist to be living inside this or any candidate. It is to see if they have any sensitivity to the injustice that still pervades humanity in general. And whether it is likely that they will strive to improve justice wherever they can over the course of their political day/life. Or will they either ignore the reality of pervasive injustice or even perpetuate or exacerbate it with high-sounding rhetoric or self-serving political policy?

But hold on. How much justice do we really want? Who is there now that has not benefitted from injustice? Sarah Chayes, in <u>Thieves of State</u> (Norton: 2016), has boldly and thoroughly described how corruption is already close to stealing several democracies in the world. Is ours not far behind? Are we not complicit in the unfolding of historical events that exploit some and excuse others?

What other justice issues can be pursued with our candidate in a public forum? Maybe income inequality between various genders and ethnic groups? Those in power who remain silent about the environmental consequences of current levels of material waste? Or those who ignore the children and the desperate adult lives involved in the incessant jousting over the gnarly issue of abortion?

Justice was probably the first virtue identified, going back at least to Hammurabi. He felt compassion for the insensitivity of people to one another and began the human social function of regulation to try to improve the situation. Dozens of email scams per day on our computers ought to convince us that seeking justice with very little success still takes up annoying amounts of energy. Infected police departments and judicial systems, shameless marketing ploys, exploitive lawsuits, hypercomplex tax laws, and the rich constantly getting ridiculously richer while more and more people sink deeper into poverty – these are the justice issues that never go away.

We voters should eventually want a government made up of people who can be trusted. Voters hopefully want to believe that those elected top officials will give us and everybody else the best shot at fairness. We are obviously more concerned about getting our own fair treatment, but there seems to be a growing group who favor a fair society in general as well. Are we convinced that if a congress, cabinet, committee, or a leader of any of these has a basic sense of justice, that group and the government will gradually do its best to legislate and govern relatively justly? This ought not to be easily assumed as it often has been in previous elections. Remedial work of improving systems towards greater justice starts with each individual candidate. Can justice be spotted in a candidate's self-presentation? Here is an example of how the public engagement could unfold.

A candidate appears for a televised national town hall. Near the beginning of the open session, a voter calmy asks: "Sir/Ms., What is your understanding of Plato's insistence that the virtue of justice is necessary in the heart and behavior of anyone aspiring to major public office?"

After a few sentences of response, the same, or another voter asks, "How do you see your own commitment to justice as a political leader, especially relative to such ingrained systemic injustices as racism and gender wage gaps? How have you sought even small steps towards greater justice regarding those issues in your career?" "How would you do so in the current societal turmoil if elected?" Or "What is the story of the best you have done working for justice regarding any individual in need or any of our country's gnarly public issues?"

Follow-up questions by other voters will be highly important so that the impression of being confronted by an entire community is clearly demonstrated.

Justice, the evolving pursuit of fairness everywhere in humanity, goes on and will for some time to come – at the plodding pace of most lines of evolution. The natural situation of evolving human beings of all different cultures, geographies, and governing configurations meeting one another face to face in the past few centuries results in unavoidable conflict, with some always feeling treated unjustly. National leaders have as part of their positional responsibility to constantly address injustice with hopes of improving specific situations, knowing that total justice for all is currently impossible. It is important not only where we are with justice but which way we are moving and how we can vigorously continue progress. The question then becomes, "How will this candidate swim as a national leader in that complex river of injustice?" Vigorously upstream or going with the flow of apathy, sliding back? Do they indeed have inside them that persistent commitment to getting as much fairness as they can for as many as they can? That is the utilitarian view of the virtue of justice. Where is their authentic sadness in the pains about that ongoing saga of constituents pining for a fair society?

We are left with the task of finding people who already honor justice as an ideal and work for it persistently, wherever they can, while also addressing all the other communal and inter-communal problems as well. Indeed, we voters have a responsibility to sort out the potential of would-be leaders genuinely dedicated to justice and support those people for leadership.

A final example: (Ms. or Mr. Candidate), "Advocacy is a 'going with' and 'speaking for' another who is more powerless than oneself. Can you tell us one story about how you have advocated for justice for another person or group in need?"

2. Humility - Relatively Accurate Self-Appraisal

The very meaning of the word Islam is *submission*. Devout Muslims bring their minds to surrender several times a day, to Allah, what they traditionally call that power beyond us all so evident in the natural world. Christian monk Bernard of Clairvaux (1090 – 1153) wrote that "the three most important virtues are humility, humility, and humility[x]", and believed that without humility, there is no true spirituality[xi]. In AA, humility (often not by that name) is the very First Step to recovery, overcoming the arrogant grandiosity of stubborn self-reliance that keeps one stuck in the deadly secrecy of chemical dependence. In that situation, humility is the shocking realization that one is powerless over a simple chemical substance. It is acquiring the ability to admit that you are not God authentically but solidly powerless over alcohol and become unmanageable when you consume it, any of it. That realization easily leads to depression, a hard place to live, even for a while. Still, you come to see that you are no better nor any worse than anybody else on the planet in worth and value. No sobriety endures without a measure of real humility, often as a brand-new major feature of your personality.

Devout Muslims grow up with that, as do classical Catholics, Hindus, and Jews. There are many, however, who grow up understanding something about religion but not really incorporating it into their soul. One self-help author puts it well:

"Humility is…..the ability to keep one's talents and accomplishments in perspective, to have a sense of self-acceptance, an understanding of one's imperfections, and to be free from arrogance and low self-esteem." Janis Abrahms, "Spring" in How Can I Forgive You?

Humility is a component of awe, that quickly and fleetingly overwhelming sensation of being little in the face of something very, very big, like the ocean, a mountain, a Clydesdale, or reflecting on the smiling face of your daughter or son or grandchild. The deep experience of humility makes you realize that you are not so big after all. Could you make one-millionth of any of those magnificent natural world entities yourself, even a single living tree or even one living leaf? Yet you may be highly prized by somebody. Humility, like many virtues, "stands in the middle" between extremes of self-aggrandizement on the one hand and self-denigration on the other.

In clinical pastoral education circles in hospitals, addiction treatment, and hospice situations, humility as a virtue (astute self-awareness) is actively identified by the capacity to accurately appraise yourself to others, neither exaggerating your excellence nor minimizing it. In chaplain certification, it is the ability to talk about yourself, both strengths and limitations, in some depth without much exaggeration, minimizing, or reflexive goofy humor. It is tested by seeing a person describe their strengths and weaknesses as a person and as a caregiver in a small peer group with all eyes on them accurately enough so that the group peers nod in agreement and validate them verbally.

Acting sadly as if you are the worst and most miserable failure in the jail or drug treatment program is not humility. It is false pride. In politics, humility is the deep recognition of your own egotism and times of phonily behaving as if you are superior to most others. Humility allows you to collaborate simply and clearly, human to human, with other fine individuals for the good of people. Why collaborate with anybody if you believe you are the greatest?

A person with any measure of humility is likely to balk at a hyper-partisan milieu worsening in Congress and feel (secretly) ashamed of the air of superiority that often seems to pervade there. I would wager that a research study of the reasons why people leave Congress would show that prominent among those reasons is the discomfort and, eventually the disgust at the pointless audacity all around them when there is so much work to be done. The subtle, and sometimes obvious pretense that one is far more insightful, savvy, privileged, or well-intentioned than one's peers, and indeed one's constituents, seems to completely lack humility by any definition or understanding. Humility is partially visible, and so is its absence.

Public indicators that a person possesses a measure of humility start with their tone and pace when talking with you. "Fast talkers" are often quietly avoided by genuinely humble people, for good reason. More likely indicators that a person has a bit of humility include eye contact that feels connected to you as a person, willingness to address your questions seriously after carefully hearing their substance, and a "lingering with you" feeling you get when they converse with you or an entire room full of diverse adults. The ability to talk about one's own personal weaknesses and strengths without hyperbole or jocular humor remains essential and maybe the best indicator of the presence of true humility.

Remember, these are only *indicators*, not diagnostic certainties, which may not even exist regarding virtues.

To assess the suspected humility in a candidate its depth and breadth in their personality, one could ask pointed questions in a public forum. Some of these might start simply like, "How would you describe yourself as a person? As a political leader?" As they answer, notice whether there is a moment when you sense a tone of superiority.

Again, these are a different kind of question because they have a different purpose: to crack open ordinary conversation or political rhetoric, to expose the deeper recesses of this human's character, that is, a reasonable accurate understanding of themselves. Follow-up questions based on observers' perceptions of the response may include a personal comment on the first response, such as, "You sound pretty confident, Sir/Ms." Their response to that may be telling.

In a small group assessment session, more challenging questions may be in order. When you hear that grandiose tone, your simple, calm comment, "You know, that comes across to me as feeling superior, sort of beyond confidence, almost grandiose." Then wait. It may be difficult to envision such a group moment. However character cannot be assessed without accessing emotions. That is a primary fact that has been missing. It is necessary to broach it now at times, even before the establishment of small group assessment processes. And "you can't make an omelet without breaking some eggs."

In the future small group character assessment project (See Chapter Six), one would consider even more confronting comments and questions like, "What you just said sounded like it had a tone of superiority. Do you really think you are better than (Muslims, immigrants, women, etc.)"? Then wait.

Another tack, in that eventual small group, could be: "What have you done in your leadership career to assist the plight of marginalized people?" Wait. Listen carefully for the tone. Or even, "Do you think the majority of American people want another national leader who cannot empathize with downtrodden (or disadvantaged or marginalized) people?" Then, "Do you see yourself as superior to these (or some of these) people here listening to you right now?" Or "Will you tell us about a congressperson (or president or vice-president) who strikes you as acting superior?" "Do you know the difference between kings and congresspersons?" "Can you describe that difference for us"?

3. Integrity - A Solid Habit of Telling the Relevant Truth

Can you enjoy playing golf with someone you know secretly cheats on the scorecard? Maybe. But you may not trust them far in other aspects of life when the "chips are down." The country is presently facing a battering of the truth on many fronts. Many of those facades will fade in small group dynamics. Those that don't will likely blare dysfunction in the face of the savvy assessors.

Shared experience constitutes the primary way by which we connect personally in this human race. We talk. We verbally share experiences, emotions, attitudes, perceptions, convictions, and whatever else comes to our minds that is of any importance to us at all. We describe what we see, think, hear, value, feel, want, aspire to, and dream about. We sing inspiration into one another, dance up positive energy, discuss favorite novels and movie stories, loosen one another with a bit of wine, and play with our children. Most everything that "inspirits" us is a sharing of something from somewhere between our casual experience and the depths of our souls. And words play a major part in our success at doing so for a fulfilling life.

We humans thrive on physically sharing one another's bodies in intimate loving, mixing our own best interests with the hopes, fantasies, and dreams of a lover. We communicate to dispel loneliness, be understood, join efforts, get attention, and build community together. It is how evolution moves forward now that there are beings who can decide and shape the very direction of the evolutionary process[xii]. *That makes it sacred, to tell the truth whenever we can.* Obfuscation, exaggerating, minimizing, or otherwise manipulating to better our image, rationalize our intentions, sell something, or gain a material advantage – and even sloppiness in important communication – all rip at this stage of the very core of evolution.

The early Hebrews were some of the first humans to put that fundamental responsibility into the written word. Attributed to Moses, the translated words so familiar to all Christians were, "Thou shalt not bear false witness against thy neighbor." In disputes between ancient people who lived close to one another, ordinary conflicts and the urgency to get one's way in things small and large pushed them (and us) to shade the truth. The Hebrews and various others were learning that abandoning the truth in small ways leads to ever bigger deceit and eventually erodes any trust in the community. In fact, lying was recognized as one of the primary ways of behaving that prevented the communal peace for which they yearned. Being loyally truthful was making its initial ascension. For the hope of eventual serenity, they would need to consistently represent events accurately. It has taken now several thousand years to bring us to where we have enough command of language to do that—be clear, be precise, be correct, be truthful. But will we?

As a diverse nation, we still fall short of willingness. When I was five years old, our car got hit by another one, and Dad had to appear in court.

He told us about it. I only remember one thing he said. In response to being pushed about the truth of what happened, he said firmly, "… because it's too damned small a matter to lie about." To a five-year-old, that stuck. As a culture, we still don't insist on honesty, even in our court system, where winning and financial advantage can be far more valued than honesty. Indeed, lawyers imply in court that when a person lies once, they are a liar; they are not to be trusted again at all. That ploy is outrageous because of the bending of the truth that blares on all sides in the manipulative and coercive interchanges of court interactions.

We don't see much reverence for the truth in business, where image and profits stand above honest descriptions of products and fashioning readable contracts. We don't' consistently see honesty even in religion, where church attendance is often seen as a subtle "sell" for the biggest crowds.

Where there are high emotional or material stakes involved, shading the truth often just gets a nod.

Public figures, however, need to be even more careful with the truth in serious matters than those of us in the background of society. More depends on it. The well-being of millions depends on facts and facing the truth about them. We have always needed honest politicians. Now more than ever. The so-called "big lie" may have set us back decades in pursuing a community that can trust one another at their word. The best place to start is to assess the honesty component of the character of our top leaders before we elect them.

It is quite clear, even to casual observers, that a segment of national leadership has placed several of their values above their own integrity. For the sake of money, approval from party leaders, and escape from the embarrassment of losing on a highly visible legislative or electoral issue, shading the truth seems to be an easy choice. The practice of that segment of leaders is to say whatever works or remain strategically silent to remove themselves from negative exposure, like a second-grade rascal caught without his homework. To some, the brief but pleasurable titillation of stark attention from anyone suffices as a response enough to feed on until the next opportunity to elicit it occurs. That is not acceptable to any ethic-seeking society. The truth is not doing well in our world, and we are allowing it

Denials of what was proved to have happened are so slickly presented by some leaders to gain or keep their office and its privileges that we no longer trust much of what we hear anywhere. That erosion of public trust is so egregious and endemic that it would take years, probably decades, to heal. Our best tack may be to fashion approaches to sorting out candidates by catching and confronting them publicly at their colorful exaggerations, outrageous denials, and charming distortions repeatedly, calmly, and persistently before we ever decide to elect them.

We also must believe that many ingrained liars, when repeatedly confronted with obvious facts, will appear foolish in public with too much light shining on them. Will those continuing to hang on with fingernails to the cliff edge of the so-called "big lie" ever come to regret it as having stolen their integrity in politics and the country?

There is currently no predictable forum for confronting candidates in the ways necessary to sort the functional leaders from the charlatans. We will need to create such arenas. The future of our country may depend on it. Indeed, if we do not face this crisis of the truth, anything else we do to improve our national leadership will probably have little positive effect. How can a reverence for the truth be recognized in candidates by confrontations in public venues?

The fairy tale, "The Boy Who Cried Wolf," the stories of George Washington's cherry tree and Abe Lincoln's long walk to return a penny that wasn't his, injected a valuing of honesty into many of us as children. Highlighting radical honesty by national leaders helped many post-toddler agers begin to realize the consequences of lying, especially if their own verbalized untruths are met with serious family and teacher disapproval.

Opportunities life gives us from childhood to learn that lying is generally destructive in some way seem to be universal. But those opportunities are not always taken. The hot experience of being shamed and embarrassed when caught red-handed in a lie seems to be almost necessary to learn to distinguish lies from truths. We all seem to carry at least one story about that transformation in our childhood, though most of those stories are never told. Indeed, some there are who don't remember that event or have blotted it completely from their minds. And for some people, it never happened, perhaps due to family dysfunction. The mixture of truths and lies then remains hovering near pathological for a lifetime.

So how to address a potential leader in small group assessment projects about their commitment to persistent honesty? We could begin by asking politely, "How did you feel about the "big lie," as it has been called since 2020, and what did you do in response to it?" Or begin with a more general question like, "How important is it that a public leader avoid shading the truth for their own benefit?"

Another alternative might be, "Do you have a family story, Ms. ZZZ, that depicts how you began to realize the importance of telling the truth?" Then, in response to the answer, "How do you see that learning challenged by your experience in the political arena so far?" "How do you feel in the constant pressure to pretend much of the time in public politics?" More generally, in a small character assessment group, "Could we start this part, Sir./Ms., by asking you to speak openly about your convictions regarding the way the truth is treated so casually in our court system, and sometimes in Congress?" That and some follow-up questions could almost force them to face their own possibly disingenuous behavior designed to make themselves appear right, righteous, and strong, to help themselves "win" in some way, or at least appear to.

Not all events of either public or private confrontations of candidates about the truth will be dramatic. But sharp public questions will serve their purpose of gradually changing the ethics and effectiveness of our politician selection process and those who apply for it. It is pointed to questions like these, put to candidates in assessment, which demand the decision of whether to begin looking carefully at their disingenuous behavior or continue to perpetuate it, knowing that their purported facts are juxtaposed to reality. Over a short time, we can expect that consistently taking this tack will alert candidates to the need to be more careful with the truth.

4. Dedication to Humanity – A Basic Inclination to Contribute to the Evolving Human Race

What is this candidate's motivation for running for national office? That question needs vigorous attention in every case. Psychiatric theorist Harry Stack Sullivan quipped that the test of your motivation is what you actually do. Does this person place themselves in nomination seeking financial security, the esteemed place in society, to fill a great need for vigorous attention from people, or something else? Do they even know their own primary motivation? Motivation is partially visible, and if there is no deep and genuine inclination to function in that office to contribute to the betterment of humanity, it is inadequate to be allowed to continue.

A reasonably good start for a framework of prioritizing the many demands on a legislator's time and attention would be: "Which ones of those needs have the most effect on humanity as a whole?" and "Which can we possibly bring some progress to in our own nation now, so as not to lose heart and pass discouragement on to our constituents, our children, and our grandchildren"?

As the old story goes, "Two men are stranded in a small boat on the open ocean, and it begins to fill with water, listing to stern. The one at the bow snaps angrily at the other, "Your end of the boat is sinking." That scenario depicts the situation of U.S. governing bodies that incessantly blame each other, *ad nauseum*, rather than honestly seeking the leaks and collaborating in efforts to fix them. Reflexive blaming of another individual or party can stop all progress. It can be recognized partially by confrontation. It is childish. It needs to be confronted at almost every turn.

With all our American technology, research, education, and business success, we continue to fail to effectively deal with fundamental problems, including health care availability, worsening ecology presaging global disaster, relentless race relation conflicts, useless and unfair sexual orientation bias, sagging infrastructure, lack of reasonable income equality, flawed legal and corrections systems, and an overly complex and unfair tax structure. Leaders are chronically blocked by a lack of colleagueship in Congress, pandering to outrageous lobbies, and spotty wisdom in a national administration. As a nation, we need top leaders who maintain a bottom-line dedication to humanity and work reasonably to improve world living conditions. No substantive change in our national and world communal progress will occur until we have a preponderance of leaders with dedication to some version of the evolution of human-to-human mutual and communal care.

How could voters recognize such a dedication to humanity in a candidate when most of them are liable to verbally claim to have it? Indeed, many leaders may not even recognize how they honor the god of financial advancement over the happiness of all ordinary human beings. How could a town hall participant initiate a conversation about the core value of a global perspective in a candidate?

Some approaches to initiate public conversations for assessing dedication to humanity would be simply: "What is your thinking about world hunger?" That question alone deserves a bit of waiting for an answer, an opening for discussion. Expect no fluffy excuses and accept none. Other questions are for follow-up. "Whose responsibility is it to act vigorously to eradicate starvation, or at least reduce it, and continually make it a part of national governments' agendas?" "How have you thought about how a nation like ours could more vigorously address the daily pain of the half million unsheltered wanderers among us in our own country?" "What would it take for you to support initiatives like think tanks or even cabinets of half congress persons and half agricultural, engineering, and transportation experts to continually address the real problems of hunger, water shortages, trash disposal, realistic regulation of manufacturing, and environmental issues that impede human happiness?" "While these perennial gnarly human problems may never be solved, they could benefit from concerted efforts to address them as ongoing realities of society. What are your thoughts about that?" "What have you done so far in your leadership to support humanist and humanitarian efforts of governments, churches, and philanthropists focused on those values?"

And finally, active voters could address questions about philosophical issues such as the limitations of capitalism and changes that could make the planet more livable for all people. For example, "Sir (or madam), Why should there not be a limit on net worth in individual citizens as long as there are droves of hungry people on the planet?" "How does it serve humanity to have billionaires on the one hand and dreadfully indigent children on the other?" "What might the limit on personal wealth be?" "Does anybody really need more than, say for example, five million dollars in our current world?" Or even one million? "Doesn't capitalism need some restraints for the good of all people?" "Why not, except for the phony fear of the boogeymen socialism and communism?" "How would you work to reduce poverty and limit the ugliness of astonishing levels of personal capital?"

5. Fortitude – Courage Combined with Solidity

It took a few hundred million years for the animal world to develop vertebrate structures solid enough to support themselves permanently out of the water (between 550 million and 365 million years ago.) Even today, some politicians cause one to wonder if they have adequate strength in their spiritual backbone. Can they stand up to party pressures, the incessant beckoning of lobbyists' self-indulgence pandering and campaign demands to maneuver differently from what their conscience would prefer? Fortitude can best be seen as the backbone of a candidate, essential, according to Plato, for any ethical top leader.

Movie story heroes, historical or fanciful, make some of the best examples of raw fortitude. William Wallace (Mel Gibson) in Braveheart; Will Caine (Gary Cooper) and Amy Fowler (Grace Kelly) in "High Noon"; and Shane (Alan Ladd with Jean Arthur) in the movie by that name serve as bold examples. More recently, highlighting the courage and strength it takes to care deeply for others are heroines like Florence Nightingale, Mother Teresa, Malala Yousafzai, Greta Thunberg, and even such fanciful characters as Wonder Woman. You'll see the compelling virtue of fortitude boldly depicted for young boys and girls in old-time Western movies and in modern "world-saving" ones. Fortitude is the hallmark of the hero, the admired protagonist, and in today's films, the boy or girl savior of the universe.

What is now called fortitude, from the Latin "fortis," meaning both strong and brave, was identified by Hebrews, under the name of Isaiah, in describing what the Messiah (savior) would be like when he arrived (they were certain it would be a man) to finally set things straight in the world. He would not be wimpy. He would be "mighty"[xix]. Top politicians do not often need to be heroes. But they need some fortitude as persons.

Fortitude was one of the four cardinal virtues of Plato, needed in every public leader. But he used only the word "courage." The best meaning of the word today would combine courage with strength. It is the combination of the Hebrews' "mighty" and Plato's "courage". Plato considered it one of the essential virtues of a politician in an ideally ethical society. Medieval theologians saw it as a "cardinal" virtue, a hinge, one of four on which many things hang.

Whether the candidate for office is a man or a woman, they will need a solidity of fortitude to join and contribute to the world of national leaders. The abundance of this virtue is often won earlier in life by the experience of being pushed around physically, verbally, or emotionally in a dysfunctional family, bullying school class, or a "house of cards[xx]" political world of subtle coercion, innuendo, and the ubiquitous, thinly veiled, ruthless self-interest of others. Early distaste for feelings of guilt and inadequacy can be powerful deterrents from cowardice during adult life if they are seen and acknowledged clearly enough.

For the ancient Hebrews, the Messiah would have *fortitude* and all leaders need it because it is neither easy nor safe to stand and function in front of a community, no matter how wise, fierce, and benevolent you are. Any national leader with an ounce of integrity may have to stand against their peers and colleagues and pay the price for not following the party line in crucial situations. Some of your constituents will always misunderstand and keep demanding new accomplishments, blaming you for mistakes, and crying for justice on opposite sides of issues with one another.

Fortitude is on several of the historical lists of virtues (Confucius, Plato, and Isaiah, for example), presumably because it is so universally needed and in short supply. Only heroes have enough of it in some situations, and that is often because they were caught with their "courage on" in the right place at the right time. But if a person doesn't have at least a kernel of fortitude, they ought never to run for major political office. They can almost anticipate being crucified for their best thinking, convictions, and conscience if they display them.

In politics, fortitude is a kind of angry solidity that will fight ferociously and interpersonally for what a leader deeply cares about or loves. It is backed by considerable emotion that motivates tenacity, overcomes the inertia of fearfulness or laziness, and finds the verve to withstand opposition and drudgery. National leaders possess a sad dearth of fortitude when they cave in to peer pressure, legal threats, party coercion, and media twisting. If they only watch silently when their duty is to confront, challenge, and even impeach an errant leader, they are likely to be remembered as cowards, if at all, by historians and have their legacy completely ignored.

A national leader must exhibit some fortitude in their personal and professional history, and most of them do. But it seems to abandon many of them at key moments when heroes would shine. It did not do so in Liz Cheney in 2021. At high noon, alone on Main Street, she showed up, stood up, and faced the ugliness caused by the trashing of the truth. And she continued to do so long after, persistently, boldly, magnificently, and beautifully.

The color and strength of fortitude in a candidate may be seen in several ways. Is there any sign of persistence in this candidate, especially against strong resistance? What is this person's participation in conflict-filled movements and issues, such as legalizing abortion and marijuana, the death penalty, racism healing, or gun violence? Has this person ever stood against the leadership of their own party? How did they see the impeachment events of early 2020 and 2021? What did they do and say about those issues then? Can they name a time when they regret not standing for a value, in youth or in politics?

In public forums, how do they respond to critique and confrontations about their record on controversial issues? How do they acknowledge and share any history of childhood skirmishes, and for what values? Remember, in evaluating fortitude, you are not just looking for what they have stood for, but more, whether they have stood for anything with passion.

A key slant here is the obligation of a public figure to confront errant peers when necessary. In the future small assessment group, some initial questions might be, "What would it take for you to vote to impeach and remove from office a member of Congress or a president of the United States?" "What will have transpired in your attempts to confront the behavior of that errant person individually, directly, face to face, before thinking about impeachment?" "What are some of the lines that would need to be crossed by a peer national leader for you to consider solidly admonishing that person in private?"

"Have you ever been in a fistfight or semi-public shouting match?" "What was so important then?" "Will you talk with us about a time when you needed to be interpersonally forceful, persistent, and vulnerable in service of your work for a major cause or for the good of the city, state, or the country itself? What did you do to protect the basic values of humanity in that conflict?" "What is one time you confronted, in private, a peer leader about their attitudes, decisions, decorum, or questionable behavior?" "Do you now harbor any regrets about that time or its timing?". "Do you now feel proud of it?"

6. Temperance – Moderation of Attitude, Alcohol, Anger, Appetite, and Avarice

Both temperance and prudence were included by Plato in his highlighting the four cardinal virtues[xxi] needed by leaders of an ethical city, (including also courage and justice). Both temperance and prudence have the general nuance of restraining impulsiveness, the natural inclinations of people to get carried away getting their way, then called concupiscence (Latin, "eager desire" or "to long for"). While *prudence* allows a person to consider the best ways to fit ideas and behaviors into current local norms, deliberations, and emotional contexts, *temperance, here, is the virtue by which we restrain our behavior from personal excesses that distract or deter us from effectively actualizing leadership roles.* They drag down our effectiveness.

Named from the Latin *temperantia*, "to moderate," this virtue refers to being able to avoid excessive eating, drinking, procuring, and angry behavior in what has been called "having a temper." Temperance means discretion and self-control ruling over both our natural and our unique habitual impulses and excesses. Plato taught, "Temperance is *the ordering or controlling of certain pleasures and desires* [xxii] ...." A common saying of the Hellenists was from Plato[xxi], "The first and the best victory is to conquer self."

It was clear to Plato and his colleague Greek philosophers that an "ethical state" needed leaders who could resist the weaknesses inherent in humanity to govern—observe, listen, think, discern, and act— effectively.

The word temperance was made a U.S. household term in the 1920s by those pushing for prohibition, the law making the "manufacture, sale and transporting of intoxicating liquor" illegal from 1920-1933. The movement that led to prohibition was often called the "temperance movement," assumed to mean complete abstinence from alcohol for everyone, a meaning that supplanted a broader understanding of temperance prior to that. Prohibition as a law did not work at all. The population did not know then that alcohol affects some people horribly, while for most people, it only catalyzes conviviality and occasional drunkenness.

Certainly, for most people, it is enough to be vigilant about our drinking. But for the other ten percent, it is another matter. Still today, alcoholism is a dreaded label, not understood widely as an illness that can be treated. Any candidate will be cautious about being labeled an alcoholic or addict. They would need to be assured by the character assessment group that if they have lost control of their mood-altering chemical usage at some time in the past but are in a recovery place now, their history will not be disclosed to anyone without their permission. If they are currently back to "using" after a period of being treated or a time of abstinence, it is in their best interest and that of society that they do not serve until they have been living in recovery for an extended period of time, at least six or twelve months.

In a candidate for major leadership, temperance of every kind is quite necessary since the position being sought is one of great power—variously influencing military forces, fashioning and monitoring billion-dollar budgets, and access to "the button" that could initiate the nuclear war that could end all life on earth. Impulsive people ought not ever to be in that position.

Do you want your president drunk, seriously depressed, or "manic" at a crucial time?

In Congress and the White House, like anywhere else, regulation is not very effective in curtailing excessive drinking. It takes developed virtue inside a person—temperance for those who can drink normally and abstinence in recovery for those who cannot. Several presidents and numerous congresspersons have histories of a high level of drinking. Asking a few questions about the drug and alcohol use of candidates for Congress or president in the small group setting is clearly justified. The following questions would be appropriate, especially if the assessment group included an addictions counselor. "Do you drink alcohol at this point in your life?" "About how much per week?" (Watch their face during their verbal response.) "Do you ever use any other mood-altering substances, prescribed, legal or not?—marijuana, stimulants, depressants?" "Has anybody ever suggested that you might have a problem with drinking or drugs?" *"Do you at times have concerns about your alcohol use or other mood-altering chemical use?" "Do you like all of your drinking, or are there sometimes you feel concerned about your drinking behavior?" "Will you tell us about some of those times?"*

Anger, too, has its place and proportions that work. Justified anger contributes heavily to fortitude in pointed confrontation. Unbridled rage does not.

Some questions and observations in a small group context that can be useful in sorting out a candidate's temperance regarding anger and conflict would be: "Have you ever had a temper tantrum, i.e., losing your judgment and composure in angry reaction, since becoming a public figure?" "How would your friends and spouse answer that question about you?" "What kinds of things infuriate you?" "Do you know why?" "Can you give us an example of a time when you 'lost it'?" "Have you ever hit anybody or thrown things as an adult?" "What physical fights have you been in during your life?" "Will you describe one (some) of those and tell us the story?"

To probe excessive consumption of food and drink, some initial questions might include: "Will you talk about any efforts you have made to lose weight?" "Are you pleased with your own physical self-care right now?" "How do you think your overeating and problem drinking would affect your performance as a national leader?"

Regarding the temperance of money lust, the starting question could be, "How important is it for you to be rich?" (See further suggestions in Chapter Five, Thrift.)

Answers to any of these questions would not necessarily rule out candidacy for national office. But they would increase the self-awareness of the candidate and heighten their vigilance for excess, or maybe increase their level of defensiveness about it, which would be revelatory. The data of the small group assessment meetings would not be shared publicly, but a substantive, general report would identify some of the possible problems in leadership. They may also alert the country to the potential for a given candidate "losing it," becoming impaired, and unable to serve effectively due to intemperance, when in office.

7. Benignity – Consistently Seeing the Good in Situations and People

Most of us are far more familiar with the term malignancy than its opposite, benignity, due to the prevalence of cancer in the population. Leading positive psychologist Martin Seligman calls benignity "consistently seeing the good in situations and people." It was mentioned by Paul of Tarsus as one of the traits of new Christian converts, referring to such exhilarating experiences as an overwhelming euphoria at feeling forgiven by a loving Transcendent being for all harm one has ever done or responsibility neglected. Roughly equivalent to hopefulness, benignity is an overarching but quiet optimism about the universe and its evolutionary direction, as taught by Teilhard de Chardin. Short of a Pollyanna-type cheeriness, benignity is realistically a virtue that initially sees the good in people and situations, leaving room for future change in that assessment.

The *ren* of Confucius, the natural inclination of all people to protect children who are hurting or in danger, parallels the virtue of benignity in early Christian virtue writing[xxiii] , which carried a similar meaning without the specific reference to children. Both words similarly convey the meaning of quality in a person by which they *instinctively sense what is good in a situation and honor it with words and actions*. This is an attitude that is maintained to a considerable degree even after being disappointed, deeply hurt, or betrayed by another person, group, or society.

Conscience is the internal sense that we have acted, or are about to, without benignity or have neglected to act when a painful situation called for it. As human beings, most of us seem to be naturally benign rather than malignant, following a path in any situation that benefits humanity as a whole—until we don't. That instinctive guide to benefit humanity can be muted inside us by our own painful early life experiences, how we have been mistreated, misused, mis-taught, and misguided, a basic insight of Freud that included the genius concept of transference.

It is important that this natural *ren* in a candidate has not been seriously muted or has been substantively healed of the scars of the past before that candidate is granted a major leadership position. We, voters, ought to be able to expect our top leaders to sense goodness even when it is obscured by apparent woundedness. Responding to suffering people with confronting comments at times constitutes a caring decision, a side of what is meant by "tough love," doing the best one can to actively care for people who are still stuck in self-defeating behaviors, such as siblings, children or parents still wreaking havoc due to their addictions to anything, or mere stubborn repeated trashing of people they care for.

The language of virtue, especially benignity, may sound naïve to an experienced politician. That may be because current politics so easily translates every issue into the language and thinking of power dynamics – winning, dominating, forcing, controlling, commanding, coercing, acquiring, being right, and ruling. Maybe increasing the number of women in politics, which is certainly happening, will eventually improve that overfocus on the hard side of human relationships. And maybe not. Women can act outrageously, too, and be fearfully passive as well.

In general, congeniality would be a better approach whenever it can be implemented. Granted, compromise cannot always be employed. But consistent collaboration requires it often, and confrontation as well. That hope is embedded in such sayings as "You can catch more flies with honey than with vinegar." For now, our leaders need some of both benignity and informed fortitude. Does this candidate have them?

Sorting out the hints of major malignancy of a candidate in a small peer group would remain a minimal but essential requirement when that level of character assessment is designed. The assessment group commits to do that, if nothing else. More likely, the task is to see if the group can find a substantial measure of the elements of benignity—sensitive compassion, conveyed empathy, and skilled kindness—within the session, which is appropriate for this candidate. Benignity and kindness can be claimed publicly by a person and still be mostly absent inside.

No virtue assessment is completely accurate. But the evil historically perpetrated by top leaders who lack this basic virtue is legendary, even in present times, in several countries in the world. That justifies being careful in assessing benignity as a real and operant virtue in candidate appraisal. A kind or warm tone of voice remains an indicator of a benign character. But it can be feigned, and likewise, the faking itself can often be sensed by a careful listener.

The concept of "tough love" seems to have originated by Bill Millikin in a book by that name in 1968, referring to how teenagers at risk of homelessness and being lost for life in self-sabotaging behavior need very difficult decisions made about them for their own welfare. The term tough love was subsequently used by addiction treatment specialists and by people familiar with the courage needed by the family and friends around an alcoholic person or another addicted one. The notion of doing what an addicted person needs, not what they want and expect, can be excruciating if you love that addict. Benignity is sometimes so elusive and the opposite of what seems kind. But it is the only tack that works in many cases. That will be true too for confronting a politician who is functioning without benignity and other essential virtues and cannot see their own self-defeating behavior as they govern or are distracted from doing so.

Making the determination of benignity in a large group can start with asking: "Do you think the majority of people mean well in their interactions with other people most of the time?" "Will you tell us of a time when you have given a struggling stranger the 'benefit of the doubt' in meeting them?" "When is the last time you can remember being creatively kind to your spouse or intimate partner?" "How do you see the difficulty this country has had with immigration reform?" "What do you think should be done with that conundrum?" "How do you understand both sides of the abortion standoff?" (Is there kindness in the voice when they describe the positions of both sides?) Combining benignity with fortitude remains a major challenge for all of us. But it will be necessary to eventually change the world of politics on some issues.

8. Charity–- Authentic Care in the Moment

Who could have the gall to raise the concept of kindness in a public forum, questioning it as a feature of a candidate's character? Yet charity and love are taught as the central virtue of Christianity and valued by all other major world religions. Shouldn't a political candidate be able to show care for a given person who is in personal pain at almost any time?

Besides possessing a sturdy "strong side" of their personality in fortitude, a national leader also needs to nurture a genuine "soft side," a human side, a warm part of them that identifies with the powerless, the marginalized, the youngster, and the unsheltered, right in their midst. And can they convey empathy to a given person in this present moment? If not, how can they lead fairly, with a persistent effort at improving justice and care for anybody hurting? Compassion of heart is one thing, but it is internal. Showing it with kindness in needed words and actions is quite another.

To be expected to demonstrate the ability to show empathy and compassion to a given individual in a public situation would put many politicians in a very tight situation. Accustomed to brandishing a sharp, smoothly verbal, and knowledgeable image to the public, being asked to shift into an intimate and authentically compassionate expression of immediate, personal care requires considerable flexibility of one's personality. But raising kindness as a virtue in a public forum does send a signal that the harsh, disingenuous values that seem ingrained into US politics need not stay that way. If voters are seen as closely watching characters, then candidates being assessed need at least a disapproving glance and a hint that lack of kindness boldly demonstrated by observed actions of national leaders will not be tolerated for very long.

In short, can this candidate be kind right now, at this moment, in this public forum? We're somewhat interested in whether they can claim kindness, even tell stories of having been kind at times in their life. But can they care verbally for one of the people gathering here and now? The moderator might choose one among attendees with a recent major loss and ask the candidate to take a few minutes to offer solace now. A leader who cannot be intentionally kind to almost anybody they meet would best be looked at more carefully about their promise of caring responsibly for a nation.

Observed kindness is purported to have been the difference noticed strikingly in early Christian converts that compelled others to embrace that movement too, in huge numbers, across the Mediterranean, in Christianity's first 200 years. It is still the very core value of Christian belief, though sometimes overshadowed in organized churches by faith, compliance, and financial generosity. For Hindus, too, there is the quote, "When a person responds to the joys and sorrows of others as if they were his own, he has attained the highest state of the spiritual union" (Bhagavad Gita 6.30320). And in Islam, there is: "Worship Allah and associate nothing with Him. Be kind to parents and near kindred, and to the needy, and to the neighbor who is near and to the neighbor who is a stranger, and to the friend at your side, and to the wayfarer…." (Al Nisa 4:36)

Kindness is one of those virtues that can be easily recognized episodically by its absence. Unkindness can be noticed quickly. In a public figure, we can feel it by actions that seem to ignore unfortunate people's needs, misunderstand their pleas, and condemn them for their pathos. All of us have been unkind, and some of us very seriously so. A candidate for office could well be asked, "What is a time you regret when you were sharply unkind to someone? Was it ever somebody under your leadership, supervision, or care?" Their response would be a test of openness as a person.

Episodes of unkindness are how people lose their benignity or how it is recognized that a person is not so benign. When a leader is nasty in a situation that does not seem to call for a hard side comment or action, onlookers will typically try to overlook that event and excuse it if the onlooker likes the leader and condemn them internally if they don't. Kindness is best if it is observed as a person's habit, not just a complaint or a showy effort that is episodically contrived. The tone of voice often tells the tale.

Clearly and softly conveyed, empathy is a genuine art that is learned precociously by some children, only in adulthood by some of us, and never learned at all by some citizens, both men and women. It means being able, much of the time, to "create space" in time to show a person that you "get" what they are feeling when listening to them talk. A staple of some professions, it is also indispensable in intimate loving, parenting, and close friendship. It takes concentration, sensitivity, heart, and some skill to fashion responses that accurately show you hear the emotion being expressed by another person. There are several books dedicated to this kind of listening and they help prepare the leader to learn this skill, which is only grasped by practice. Good intentions and even heart-felt care *inside* are not enough.

9. Counsel – Initiative and Openness in Seeking Needed Input

One of my sons was a high school varsity swimmer. At one point, he saw me swimming the old-style backstroke and offered feedback, "You know, dad, you stop in the water after every stroke. It would be lots more efficient if you would alternate using one arm at a time." I was in my sixties at the time, and now, years later, I still use the old backstroke, believing that what I need at my age is steady, consistent exercise, not efficiency and speed. His way wears me out quickly. There is no right way. It's a matter of asking for various diverse perspectives and then making the final decision yourself. Collaboration regarding your own important decisions, personal or professional, is the virtue of counsel. Its origins are at least as old as the Old Testament prophet Isaiah, who used the Hebrew word. Counsel's history passes through the centuries of religious order traditions, the Catholic confessional, and medical practitioners, and now has a vital existence in psychotherapy, counseling, clinical supervision, and even close friendships found and fashioned by a few trusted individuals. Consulting goes both ways, with the consultor trusting enough to be open about their troubling inner experience and the consultant listening to the consultor objectively and carefully, following up with providing feedback validating what they like and asking good questions about what they don't. It sounds complicated, but it is an intimate exchange to get better clarity on something confusing and worrisome to a person.

The richness of the virtue of counsel is a brave ability to request and listen to your peers and other experts when you need to, now called "seeking consultation." A political leader can't know everything about everything, so they had better be able to listen to those who have the key current knowledge necessary to understand an individual pained person or group. Presidents have counsel built in from staff, cabinet members, secretaries, and content leaders of all kinds. But it still takes humility to continually develop counsel, this ability, and especially willingness to humbly ask savvy peers and experts for advice and input on decisions without giving away their right and responsibility to make that final decision themself.

The virtue of counsel doesn't come naturally to very many people and doesn't come easily for almost anyone without learning from some dreadful experience that resulted from their own excessive self-reliance. The medieval monastic vow of obedience requires discernment regarding who you listen to while making serious decisions. Monks agreed to use the temporary leader of their monastery in that way. Sometimes, it was helpful. But there might have been savvy peers who would have been more perspicacious and more precisely experienced who could have helped them more if they had asked. Choosing quality peers for consultation is a big part of the art of consulting.

It should go without saying that the national leaders of a reasonably successful democratic country routinely collaborate to make decisions for the good of the people. But without a measure of the virtue of counsel in key members, that process of negotiation and compromising becomes maddeningly dysfunctional. Counsel is what allows a person to talk openly about what they are considering, proposing, or working on, and then listen carefully to chosen colleagues who respond with good questions, clarifications, suggestions, or even astute confrontation.

This virtue is mostly shown only in private. Not everybody has the maturity to accept that a public leader isn't always sure about all issues. But dualism and partisan collusion seem to have narrowed or even replaced the virtue of counsel in Congress and the White House in many instances.

This collaborative virtue thrives on having the willingness and skills to ask privately for significant help when the time comes that we need it, and to give counsel to others when they need it. It includes the ability to do so in a way that optimizes the likelihood one will get a valuable response – asking the best persons to consult with you, using a tone of genuine humility, openly describing your need, willingness to listen to the opinions of consultants, and earnestly considering whether to follow what is suggested. Some practitioners of professional helping disciplines don't mature or even survive in quality practice without getting such consultation prescriptively if not frequently.

High-level leaders presumably do better for the country when they learn how and when to get a consultation. The "how" and the "who" are the bumps. The word 'consult' comes from the Latin 'con' or 'with,' combined with *sultare*, "to strike,' resulting in "to strike together." For candidates to 'strike together' regarding public issues, they will have to collaborate, negotiate, and compromise for the success of serving diverse people's needs. The skills and attitudes of consulting should be required for holding those positions.

That is particularly true of consulting with peers who support another side of an issue. Currently, politicians may do well in eliciting feedback and advice from peers of the same persuasion. But when they begin to genuinely seek consultation from those with opposite views, things will often flow deeper and more efficiently in Congress.

Getting counsel is only done with humility. Otherwise, it is mere posturing, avoiding the soul. Genuinely asking for help can be most difficult from a leadership position. When you are a leader, seeking help from your colleagues can make you feel vulnerable to the judgment of people who always expect strength and confidence from you. Help from those of quite different political positions multiplies that fear. Group consultation from diverse peers of similarly interested but variously opinionated people, such as a task force or a committee, becomes far more complicated and needs more sophisticated skills and disciplined calm. Maintaining your human-to-human stance in that role of consultation-seeker stretches anybody who tackles it.

"Love your enemies, for they tell you your faults." Ben Franklin

It is difficult to consult in a small group, even more so in a large one. Some of us would say from experience that when consulting in a group, focus your attention on those in the group you trust the most and mostly ignore those who have given indication that they don't particularly care about you until they come forth with cogent wisdom about your issue. It allows you to be vulnerable and open to benign suggestions and ignoring hostile ones while also maintaining your dignity and poise. There is an art to getting good consultation that is priceless when one achieves even a small bit of competence in doing so. But the feeling of being exposed and vulnerable to hurt from pointed, authentic feedback never goes away. Your consulting group might, after all, summarize that about this issue, you are totally wrong!

Assessing the virtue of receiving counsel in a candidate can start with any of several questions. For example, "What is the best advice you have ever gotten from a colleague?" "How did it happen that you received that consultation?" "What did that perhaps painful input you weathered mean to you?"

"What is the most successful collaborative work you have done?" "Why do you think working together in that way was so satisfying?" "Will you take us through how you have negotiated well in a critical situation?"

"What do you do well when negotiating or compromising?" "When have your limits of compromise been exceeded?" "How did that feel, and what did you do?" "Who was your best colleague ever?" "Why did that seem to work so well?" "What was your part in working so effectively with someone?" "Who has been your most challenging colleague or peer to work with?"

*　　*　　*　　*

These nine virtues stand as key characteristics for maintaining a genuine collaborative spirit. Until further theory and research confirm that these virtues are what make up a collaborative spirit, we can assume that we are looking for the right characteristics when we assess candidates for their collaborative spirit. As voters, then, we are looking for candidates who seem to us on careful evaluation, to have a developed sense of fairness, know themselves reasonably accurately, genuinely treasure the truth, are dedicated to the human community, not merely to the nation and themselves, have the backbone of an adult, can be intentionally kind, are fundamentally hopeful, have a handle on their weaknesses, and are not afraid to get consultation often, having developed the skills to benefit from it. From one point of view, a tall order to find. From another perspective, however, it is what we ought to prefer and seek from leaders pursuing positions that wield such power.

Chapter Four:

A Fullness of Character in Top Leaders

We have described a collaborative spirit in pragmatic virtue terms. In general, legislative collaboration will be enabled by leaders who possess enough of that worldview as a primary component of their personality. But it will not be enough. More characteristics will be needed for a top leader to function effectively in their specific role in the government. A cook, for example, who has developed the personality traits necessary to work with the chef and all their kitchen and restaurant colleagues still must know how to cook and keep learning new skills, recipes, ingredients, brands, and culinary processes. Politicians, too, even if they are effectively committed and skilled to be collaborative, need to activate sophisticated other aspects of their personalities to serve the people they represent functionally. Many of these developed capacities for leading in Congress and the administration have been identified by their forbears in virtue terms. There are at least nine.

Savvy: The Integration of Knowledge, Understanding, and Wisdom

This trio of virtues mentioned separately in Hebrew writings of the eighth century BC,xxiv stand together relative to a candidate's cognitive/affective ability in leadership. Does this potential candidate show the savvy it takes to put together facts and concepts about what they know, with their personal understanding of diverse peoples, into a wisdom of seeing innovative perspectives that have the possibility of working well in many given instances? How often, when commenting on a boss, manager, or public official, are the words used, "They don't know what they are doing?!" or "They don't understand what it's like to be us"! Those all-too-common events indicate there is a missing component of political savvy in some measure in this person. How are these three – knowledge, understanding, and wisdom – related? First, the term knowledge, in general, means practical and theoretical awareness of a subject or person gained by education or experience.

As a political virtue, knowledge is a rich familiarity with the facts, organizational policies, procedures, and functions necessary to operate effectively in a specific area of life and work. It is a common expectation for public leaders that they know and accept the overall purpose of this government, the bare history of perennial problems, which of the groups they govern might be helped by a decision, and which are likely to be hurt by it, on top of being very familiar with the way the branches of government are designed to collaborate in contending with one another.

There is little wisdom without knowledge. A leader needs to learn a great deal about an issue and the people it will affect before deciding what stance to take on it. Even in a digital age and beyond, top leaders will need to do a lot of reading and consulting. Artificial intelligence (AI) can organize and crunch an incredible amount of data, but the human element needs to prevail and honor the connections between us humans as primary. While robots can be programmed to be somewhat virtuous, evolution will continue to favor intimate connection, friendship, carnal loving, parenting, and the innumerable other treasures of being people dedicated to the further development of the community. That victory over our own inventions will continue to take more and more human understanding of one another and savvy regulation by leaders.

Secondly, as knowledge increases, so can *understanding,* which is the basis for wisdom. Can any politician today be expected to have much wisdom, or even understanding, about such gnarly issues as how abortion, birth control, and sexual orientation affect their constituents without having considerable knowledge about both men and women, as well as those differences between them? Will the growing number of female legislators augment growing understanding, or will it perpetuate the tension from those differences that seem endlessly complex due to persistent assumptions rather than knowledge about the complexities of gender identity?

As a society, we still seem quite stuck in fulfilling our obligation to find partial solutions to basic problems based on the emptiness of knowing what we constantly ignore. The common excuse, for example, for not regulating combat firearms in public is that regulation won't stop gun violence. That seems blind to the fact that we can't stop any kind of murder, yet none of us would want the law against it obliterated.

Anti-intellectualism still abounds. But without personal knowledge, there is little understanding, and thus, even less positive effect of law. "Knowledge without justice ought to be called cunning, not wisdom," wrote Plato in The Republic. A cluster of strong opinions without knowledge, however, is called ignorance – not seeing, pretending not to see, refusing to see, or lying about what one actually sees.

There is no wisdom without *understanding,* either. Knowledge of facts stands only halfway between ignorance and understanding. "Standing under" the people who rely on you for guidance and reasonable regulation can't come without that leader listening in-depth, really hearing many people, diverse groups of them, not just a few. The ability to listen to both those organizationally beneath you, those above you, and your peers as well is the only real way to a leader's specific knowledge and understanding.

Even reading is not enough. In Spanish, there are two words for knowing. *Ser* means to know something cognitively. *Conoser* means to know it experientially. For example, *"yo se"* there is a Bulgaria and a Rio de Janeiro. But I personally *"yo conozco"* Rome, Paris, and Chicago because I've been there. Think of the long history of the obviously inhuman practice of slavery and how the integrated combination of learning for knowledge, listening for understanding, and reflecting for objective wisdom to make the best decisions possible would have saved mountains of pain if they had evolved sooner than they did in the twenty-first century. Where would we be with racism if our former leaders had been able to listen to African Americans as equally human two hundred years ago and more? Or Native Americans who got here first. Or the immigrants who harvest our vegetables. Or the women who birthed us and our children and shaped our lives. Though our leaders will never carefully listen perfectly, there is much more we can do to gradually increase the counsel of politicians by electing those who can truly listen, know, understand, and wisely collaborate. That is the way of evolution, always moving forward jerkily, leaving enormous waste and pain in its wake, right alongside a positive mutation that suddenly changes many things for the better. Rather than resent, regret, or blame anyone, including ourselves, for past atrocities and deserting neglect, we need leaders with that triumvirate of virtues – knowledge, understanding, and wisdom – to move forward awkwardly, haltingly, and at a glacial pace. But ahead. (indent) We also expect that political leaders will try to *understand* political processes and our constituents well enough to make reasonable decisions about our welfare. Is that too much to ask of highly educated leaders, well-paid, endowed for life, and privileged with high-profile social status? No, but that is not enough either. No leader can deeply understand all those they lead. But if a leader cannot listen carefully to differing points of view about gnarly societal issues, even knowing they can't please everyone, they are not yet fit to lead.

Claiming to understand without listening, for decades and even centuries results in the kind of convoluted racism issues with no clear immediate solutions found after the death of George Floyd in Minneapolis in 2020 and so many others. True listening for understanding can be a healing moment at any point in the aftermath of racist atrocities, though nothing can remove the immediate pain of the loss of people who loved them, nor the excruciating memories of those who have been similarly mistreated in the past.

Third, *Wisdom* is *the art of integrating knowledge with understanding to make uncommonly fitting decisions with imagination, insight, perspective, and vision.* So far, there is no way of measuring wisdom, nor typing, facilitating, or requiring it. It sometimes arises in people, even children, unpredictably when they know a situation with some clarity, understand some of its chief complexities, wait for wisdom to come and sit on their shoulders, and then blurt it out of their mouths. Wisdom has a life of its own and cannot be forced, required, commanded, or manufactured. Some individuals seem to be born with an abundance of wisdom and become known for it, such as the classic Greek philosophers, Hebrew leaders, and a few kings and presidents. But not many.

Wisdom includes the specific aspect of quickly finding perspective, the ability to change a person's point of view on an issue or a phenomenon by supplying a surprising perspective that appeals to a wide variety of people. Ann Landers (Ester Pauline Friedman Lederer) was arguably the most prolific and popular purveyor of practical sagacity of all time, with 90 million readers at the time she died.[xxv] Her advice was often wise, and no clear etiology or source was ever clear about where it came from.

Wisdom, however, can be mysteriously adopted from the experience of others who have gone before. In AA, there are little books written by recovering people on various topics, useful for daily reflection by people assiduously following the AA Steps and Traditions. Vestiges of pride may keep some people living with an addiction some people living with a substance use disorder from using that writing. But those who use it find that they can immediately come in contact with some of the best wisdom of others who were at one time similarly seeking recovery over the years in order to eventually improve their lives.

"Mankind will never see an end of trouble until lovers of wisdom come to hold political power, or the holders of power become lovers of wisdom." –Plato.

Wisdom can also be blocked from arriving. Sticking too closely, even obsessively, to established procedures, practice traditions, once-effective rituals, and legal precedent will not often bring wisdom. A senate majority leader may have the power to choose what issues come before the Senate, but wisdom is lost when they use that power to effectively halt any progress or even discussion of issues completely. That may be legal, procedurally allowed, and sometimes even ethical. But often, it does not respond to the needs of the people of the United States, nor is it faithful to the basic purpose of a three-part government configuration. Sly rather than wise would best describe it.

If hundreds of bills are passed by the House of Representatives only to die in wait without discussion on the Senate majority leader's desk in apparent partisan stalling, without being considered by even a Senate committee, and no options by anyone else to proceed, there seems to be a gross lack of wisdom in that aspect of government systems. If there is no way to change the system that permits that level of political manipulation, there is little hope for a reasonably productive government for perhaps a decade to come. Change in that system is stuck in a quagmire of partisanship, dualism, and outmoded procedures and protocols designed before even calculators were invented. Only wise leaders with fortitude, honesty, and justice will affect any useful change.

Assessing questions about these three virtues – knowledge, understanding, and wisdom—together in small process groups alerts candidates more clearly to what we citizens expect of them and how important their role is to us. Having to answer to quality peers in a small assessment group, the reasons for that kind of entrenched irresponsibility may be the best we can do to impress upon potential leaders, again and again, by pointed query and polite confrontation, that they are elected to serve the entire community, not just their special interests.

Assessment of this three-pronged savvy in a small assessment group can be initiated by confronting the character of those involved when there is a forum in which to do so. A voter, media official, or small group leader could begin, for example, by asking the basic question, "What is your understanding of the relationships between the three primary branches of government?" In a small group of highly intelligent and variously accomplished people awaiting an authentic answer, that question stands taller than it seems in writing. "Why are there three branches?" "How do you think that creative tension between them is working right now?" "How should they work together?" "Do you see any current problems with that collaboration?" "How would you deal with common conflicts between those three branches of government and the major crisis events that inevitably arise in the country?" "How could there be a better expectation and requirement of making decisions in a timely fashion?" Remedial education, sadly may be needed here.

When a hint of partisan blaming is noticed by a group member in the candidate's dialogue, an observation or another line of questions is in order, such as perhaps: "How do you understand what is being called the current partisan gridlock in this country?" "What would you propose to do about it?" Or "I noticed you taking a side in that comment. Would you be willing to talk a bit about the other side of that issue, which is supported by a lot of very smart people, too?" "What has been your part in the continued existence of the partisanship gridlock now so solid in our government?" "How convinced are you that the government (or Congress or administration) is being held back by one party more than the other?" "What is your best understanding of the other side of this partisan blockage of effective government?" If the person begins with a tone of blaming in their voice, a group member may interrupt and ask, "Would you start that over again and see if you can discuss this without a shred of blame for one side or the other?" Asking for a candidate's ability to see issues with at least some objectivity, perspective, and empathy would not be unreasonable.

Responses to these basic questions would no doubt lead to fascinating and useful, albeit awkward, further conversation and assessment data. Group members would learn quickly to follow their observations of the candidate's nonverbal communication, tone of voice, heightened energy, attitudes, basic assumptions, and expressed values by asking clarifying questions. Mild but firm confrontation will likely be needed to deepen awareness of the candidate's specific values and virtues of knowledge and understanding. Any wisdom displayed by the candidate ought to be validated as such. Blame is to be actively and immediately suppressed.

11. Thrift – Sensible Judgment about Resources

Every person maintains a basic relationship to the material world, the arena of things, money, possessions, or "stuff", and dreams of opulence or a solidly secure future. Material possessions normally take some time and thought to obtain and maintain, and that endeavor easily gets bloated into a preoccupation called greed. Wanting more and more for ourselves beyond what we need, or even modest excess, is a basic fault of humans. *Thrift* is the virtue that constantly counteracts that tendency towards greed at any level of financial status.

Thrift could be described as a developed pattern of *considering the (close up) limitations of resources in making decisions about spending, monitoring, planning for, and preserving possessions as a quality, fair member of a community.* Greed is shown most vividly in ignoring those limits with habitual extravagance and taking for granted the goodness of abundance. People accustomed to plenty from having grown up with wealth or having lost the memories of yearning for 'enough' in their past can simply lose their way in their pursuit of "more and more." They may have long ago bought into the now common greed assumption that if something legal makes somebody some money, it is good, or at least OK. That assumption seems to easily leak into justifying even what is illegal. Thrift is a quiet eye that notices waste and remembers in their soul that old saying, "waste not, want not," is not always obvious but mostly always true.

Indeed, observed wastefulness in a person serves as an indicator of lack of thrift in two dimensions—*personal waste* and communal or *public waste*. It is the difference between curating your own money and stewarding somebody else's. In politics, public thrift is caring for the money of society that can seem so limitless that even the word thrift sounds irrelevant. It is a virtue politicians need to have lurking somewhere inside them as they decide for constituents about policies, projects, budgets, grants, the nation's debt, and the economy in general.

When authorities discovered in April of 2021 an estimated 25,000 barrels full of toxic waste that was dumped in the ocean off Southern California in the 1920s, it illustrated how unlimited the natural world seemed to be until recent decades. Now that pollution of our water, air, earth, and even space is becoming increasingly obvious, the evil of greed can be recognized as even more destructive to humanity than anybody thought possible a hundred years ago. Leaders of some countries still show incredible inertia in meeting the urgency of remedial work on the health of the environment with any serious vigor. That includes the U.S.

Stubborn *personal* waste includes all those tasks you do irresponsibly with your own refuse and daily resource overuse. Simple, commonly mentioned thoughtless behaviors like needlessly letting water run from your faucet, trashing edible food, keeping lights on when they're not being used, running dish and clothes washing machines almost empty, unnecessary driving (and owning) of vehicles; and other neglects of extravagant consumerism, give indication of habitual personal waste. In leaders, it can be an indicator at the home of enormous corporate waste at work. Both personal and corporate waste needs to be dealt with far more boldly for our planet to survive ecologically.

Leaders who lack any realistic sense of thrift continue to lead millions of people into passivity when active thrift is the virtue needed everywhere. All national leaders need a basic eye for thrift as they carry out every aspect of their work. And government oversight entities need it abundantly.

How, then to initiate action by recognizing those applicants for national leadership who have a relatively solid penchant for thrift? How could we encounter potential leaders about their awareness of the strengths and weaknesses in their thrift?

In the large group public forum, initiating questions could be: "Sir./ Ms., Do you think it would be wise to move towards a balanced budget in our country again?" "How would we begin to do that?" "What do you think it would take to enlist all of the citizens to embrace that as a goal.?" "What would be some legislative steps to take to address corporate waste for that aspect of pulling together on addressing the country's still wasteful living habits?"

In the small assessment group context, a member could begin by asking: "Would you tell us a bit about how you curtail your waste in your home, with such things as water, food, electricity, gasoline, and money?" "What is your philosophy of responsible ecology"? "What do you say you do in following that philosophy in your home?" "How about in hotels and other public buildings?" "Where do you see the most waste in our federal government"? "Do you think Congress misses the issues of waste because of their sense of entitlement from their benefits that far exceed those of the general public?" "What are some of the initiatives and programs government leaders could implement to reduce waste and pollution in our country?" "What letter grade (A to F) would you give yourself for how you have attended to your own waste, both private and corporate so far in the past ten years? Tell us why you deserve that grade?"

12. Prudence – Circumspection with Restraint

Imprudence in leaders must have irked the Greeks as much as it does citizens of the world's nations today. The fantasy is easily generated that half of the society could govern with better common sense than some of those being chosen as top leaders. Only a tiny few of us, however, must ever face the scene of unforeseeable, enormous complexity and peril that descends upon successful candidates the day they assume the responsibilities of a nation's top executive or congressional role. They must suddenly, on that first day, realize that "I had no idea!!!...." Without already established patterns of behavior, attitude, and values, put together called virtues, top leaders have little chance of developing them in the heated stew of juggling dire issues every day while in office.

That is but another reason we desperately need to look more closely at their character, their possession of key virtues, on their way to those major posts of leadership rather than waiting to assess them after they are elected. We can call *prudence,* in this context, *discretion enhanced by public exposure* or *sagacity regarding one's conduct.* Prudence is taking a good, quick, but careful look at the moment before doing or saying something that may be offensive, hurtful, foolish, or rude. It differs in that way from wisdom, which most often is born of serious, deliberate reflection and sometimes of unexplainable immediate inspiration.

Prudence is etched into us by experience, though some seem to have it quite impressively as a natural part of their early makeup and development. For most, we need experience to shave the sharp, troubling edges off our childhood and adolescent impulsive inclinations. Without studied reflection on our actual past *faux pas,* we may not make much progress on that life learning, and by external observation, we may easily conclude that some folks never do. They ought not to govern, at least not in top national roles. Too much is at stake. Entire political directions and whole world reputations can be not only dented but crushed by bumbling, passionate, selfish, impulsive top leaders. Some have been responsible for thousands, even millions, of deaths.

The virtue of prudence can also be understood as *thoughtful caution that assesses one's raw inclinations to speak or act in a certain way.* It is a moment of hesitance before speaking or acting in public, which allows estimation of the damage that could follow, blurting their ideas and raw inclination just now. Experience embeds cautiousness as a virtue in a person until they become a good monitor of their own cogent spontaneity. It is shaped by the experience of public exposure and transforms into a virtue of good sense about the impression we make on other people. Not often a virtue of the adolescent, it stays at a fledgling level for some people all their lives. As adults, these perpetual adolescents can be verbally impulsive, chronically un-wise, and often offensive. Prudence gives us comity in groups and associations, congeniality in romance, and keeps us out of jail.

From the Latin *prudencia*, it literally means a foreseeing, an intuitive ability to make a good prediction of how acting on a certain inclination would affect them and those around them if they would implement it right now. Totally without prudence, we would be a buffoon, a rude philistine, an obnoxious fool. Prudence uses discretion and restraint to wait for another day to take a specific action we may be dying to do right now or an awkward, offensive phrase we are anxious to speak immediately.

Prudence has for a few thousand years, at least since Plato, been recognized as a core virtue that anybody publicly representing millions of people desperately needs so as not to act or speak as a dolt, a farm animal out of place, or a proverbial snake at a picnic. It should be easy to see why it is important to assess as a virtue in any candidate aspiring for leadership of a country.

The spiritual skill of eloquence can be a big help in acting consistently with prudence. The ability to find words quickly that fit a situation well keeps a person from looking bad in a tight spot. For example, as a public figure, imagine that you see somebody stick a live microphone in your face and insult you. What do you say that is proper for the occasion, which shows some fortitude, and doesn't return insult for insult? Prudence keeps us from saying what a part of us would really like to say, and eloquence gives us words to cleverly respond instead with both verve and class.

Recognizing prudence in a candidate can start in public with "What would you say was one of the biggest mistakes you have ever made in public life?" Then, "What did you learn from that event?" Indicators of a prudent adult include such observations as seeing them respond to difficult questions in measured tones with a minimum of hyperbole, referring an issue to a later time amidst pressure to make the decision immediately, having a history of making successful decisions, and use of consultation before making major decisions whenever possible.

Assessing prudence in a small group may be done spontaneously when group members see its opposite, something a candidate does or says that is clearly imprudent. But perhaps failing that, one could ask something like, "Tell us about a time when you embarrassed yourself verbally in a group or semipublic situation. What do you wish you had done instead, or after, to try to remedy the situation quickly?"

13. Tolerance and Acceptance: Bearing Failure and Aligning with Fate

The state of the world does not rest on one signed cake; one missed golf shot, or one legislative failure. In a large pluralistic society, failure is obviously a given in legislating as well as athletics, cooking, art, and most any other endeavor worth our efforts. It is how we deal with failures, small and large, that reveals a bit about our character.

A leader needs to have a realistic sense of knowing when to quit. An army fighting on and on in a losing battle only costs lives. Insisting on futile medical treatment prolongs suffering. Excessive commitment to success is most likely mere pride, image management, and costly stubbornness, as Napoleon learned in Russia. But before quitting, a virtuous politician must first tolerate many things and do it with a certain kind of suffering. It is painful for a congressperson with a collaborative spirit to see that attitude and cluster of virtues trashed on all sides. They will have to find ways to tolerate that situation because there is no quick way out of the partisan quagmire in which they are frequently now almost imprisoned.

As human beings active in the world, there are many things that we don't like because they are destructive to our values, impede goal efforts, or appall us with their depth of evil and human pain. How we meet those dreadful events makes a difference in our lives. Tolerating and accepting are two of the best ways to eventually not waste too much life energy in regret, resentment, discouragement, and the frozen guilt of remorse. In politics in an advanced democracy, legislators can learn to tolerate failure without proverbial kicking and screaming. They resist one another's points of view based on opposite convictions but know when to stop resisting. Like in basketball, there will be another rebound soon enough. Let go of this one since your opponent got it first, without regret. In art, we can seldom get a piece of our creativity so nearly perfect that we don't have regrets about it along the way. An absence of regret is a sign of choosing to live with something we don't like. That is the one face of tolerance.

Sometimes, a painful situation seems to last and last. Tolerance grows thin. Annoyance turns to aggravation, then acting out, protesting, resistance, and finally rebellion. The end of a lover relationship, without fail, brings a mess of hurt, anger, fears, and pervasive sad discouragement that can burgeon into depression. Serious regrets about what might have been are a natural part of an unfinished evolutionary world. Acceptance of the big picture is another virtue of the maturing leader.

The virtue of acceptance is finding a way to embrace such human decisions or fateful eventualities that we can't understand, can't have, can't achieve, or can't master. An evolving world continually alters one's expectations of what should be based on what happens that one can't control. It confronts us repeatedly to get in tune anew with the way things are and move on to the next challenge and blessing. That fact is represented boldly in the Christian religious artifact depicting acceptance in the famous statue of the mother of Jesus holding his dead body on her lap in the *pieta* scene. It depicts the awful tragedy of losing an only child during their peak of life and struggling to trust that some good will come of it rather than sinking into resentment and despair. That ability to work, love, and contribute to humanity despite major and painful disappointments that populate every life due to mortality that both motivates our loving and eventually limits our experience is called acceptance.

As Mary Oliver writes:

"To live in this world, one must be able to do three things: to love what is mortal; to hold it against your bones knowing your own life depends on it; and when the time comes to let it go, to let it go."

How tolerance of troubling people and tragic events on the one hand and acceptance of the limitations of human living and the facts of life on the other contribute to the productive life of a top leader can be assessed in dialogue with candidates. It can start with these tentative questions below. Again, research and human progress itself will eventually develop more efficient approaches.

"Sir/Ms., will you talk with us a bit about a major loss you have suffered and how it has affected your life direction?" "Who among those you have loved has died?" "Will you talk a bit more about that person, what they meant to you, how they died, how you said goodbye (or not), how you think of them now?" The major losses of a person's experience can tell something about their virtue of acceptance and suggest some stuck places in hostile resentment and painful regret. These are spiritual states that either buoy them up, wear them down or drain off energy in such excessive distractions as frantic overwork, relentless acquisition in greed, superficiality in self-absorption, obsessive preoccupations, and pervasive attitudes of entire groups of people in diverse cultures.

One could also ask in a small assessment group something like "Will you tell us about a dream of life you pursued as a youth, something that consolidated your yearning?" "Who else knew about it?" "What happened to that dream?" "What hopes fueled it, what 'bumps in the road' impeded it, and what eventualities defeated it, if any?" "As a legislator, do you think you work too hard to accomplish things for people, or maybe don't work hard enough to receive the pay, benefits, and appreciation from people you receive?" "What is currently disappointing to you about our government." "How do you cope with that disappointment?"

14. Reverence: Awe and Gratefulness at What is Beyond Us

The virtue of reverence is *a natural or acquired habitude of holding something or someone with the highest respect.* The word reverence is derived from the Latin verb *revereri,* meaning "to stand in awe of, to honor, to fear." The word carries a nuance of a level of fear because something—a value, a person, a truth—is so profoundly valuable that it emotionally shakes a person to encounter it. Saying you respect something doesn't mean you do. The word "respect" itself, i.e., "looking again" and again, and again, at something, implies that it is worth a lot of consideration. To gingerly sort that claim of what a candidate says they respect, one could ask, "Do you live in a way that respects the earthly environment?" "How so?" and/or listen for how they show they value it. Do they teach about it, verbally tout it, study it, or work to legislate about it?

How a person shows by behavior a solid respect for specific basic values serves as a usable measure of a person's virtue of reverence. They can be the substance of considerable dialogue with a candidate for major national leadership.

The history of religion is a chronicle of how humanity in all its iterations, ethnicities, and cultures, has coped with and enjoyed what is, beyond us all, uncontrollable, which is a viable definition of spirituality in general. Any serious reflection on the universe can hardly miss an observation that we humans are not the most powerful of all entities in creation. How a candidate has related themselves to religion's mixture of symbols, words, rituals, communities, beliefs, practices, and values is likely to give us some ideas of that person's virtue of reverence. What have they done with church, synagogue, mosque, or mandir and all that has been associated with them? It seems important that whoever is collaborating in national leadership has overcome the human penchant for either ignoring or exaggerating the emphasis on the beyond. Either extreme can skew the good sense of humility and call into question their ability to take proper responsibility for world events and not too much so. We know so little. Most of the world is still left to estimation, assessment, guess and belief.

The reason the Ten Commandments of the Hebrews have made such a contribution to virtue history is because they identified values crucial to the formation and maintenance of human communities, a major piece of the evolutionary process in our day. In essence, those ten imperatives advise that for the human community to progress, we will need to teach and practice holding in the highest reverence the values of human life, the truth, intimate relationships, parenting, personal property, self-care, and the transcendent power palpably felt in recognizing the beauty of human beings and the natural world. When you see a person spending energy on promoting those values, you are likely experiencing a person with the virtue of reverence.

Why do those values matter so much to our political leaders? Because national leadership is about community—guiding it, legislating for it, nurturing it, dialoguing with it, serving it, and listening to its constituents' critique to continually serve it better. These ten values are a practical *sine qua non* of community. They may not be its essence, but they are the elements without which the community is not likely to stand for very long. They are the perennial issues that need continued attention to make a country viable and eventually flourish. How a candidate thinks about and values these elements gives solid indication of how well they can serve in politics for the actual benefit of society. There are innumerable world views. This, of course, is not the only one. But it is arguably one of the best for humanity.

Consider, for one example, the reverencing of human life in the differing values inherent in perennial conflicts around abortion, war, gun violence, suicide, and euthanasia. They all touch into this arena of reverence for human life, and all are perennially unresolved or partially resolved political issues. They are not so much to be resolved, which may currently be impossible, but to be continually reflected on by leaders to work on discerning what is possible right now to improve them for the future.

One could introduce engagement about a candidate's reverence with: "What are some values that are sacred to you?" "How sacred is life to you Ms. candidate?" Wonder with them if they can talk about the competing values in any of today's perennial ethics conversations (listed above) or merely tout one side or the other.

What for example, are the differing views of life's value held by the two sides of the abortion issue?" "Can you describe why that issue is so perennial, as if both sides have merit?" "Can you do the same with the second amendment conflict?" "Does, for example, the right to bear arms include *any* arms by any person, at any age, in any mental condition?" "What are some of the good sense restrictions on firearms that honor our right to own weapons while better protecting our children, our peaceful society, and ourselves?" Where does the reverence of this candidate show most authentically when they talk about it?

The dualism with which public discussion, and even mention, of these issues have arisen almost to the point of making even temporary, partial improvements to them continually more difficult, sometimes seemingly impossible. They can appear to be so simple from within either side of that dualism but remain highly complex outside it. Only a government made up of mature individuals who can see both sides of an issue will succeed in finding acceptable, temporary solutions that are functional for our time, waiting to be better met in the future.

About military power: "Why do you think some people call themselves pacifists? What sense does that make to you?" "Why do we still need police forces and military services"? "Why do we need legal restrictions on their power?" "How could a congress keep a continued eye on the tension between movements to increase and decrease these huge and expensive protective military entities?" "Do we need a cabinet member dedicated to keeping peace and consistently bringing to deliberations a peacekeeping perspective, as one presidential candidate once recommended?" (Kucinich, 2002)[xxvi]

Regarding transcendence: "What moves you most deeply?" "In what ways do you nurture that part of yourself?" "Did you have a religious background as a child? "How do you look at that ideology now?" "How do you think your religious convictions, whatever they are, affect your public service?" "How do they serve you?" "How might they inhibit you at times?" How do you interpret the words of Albert Schweitzer, "Humanism in all its simplicity is the only genuine spirituality"?

About family life: "What has the term 'family values' come to mean in our society, beyond a political marketing cliché?" "Have you thought about any ways the government could better support marriage, parenting, and rearing children?" "Do you have ideas about improving education in the U.S.?"

And where is the gratefulness in all of this? Gratefulness cannot be generated very deeply by intention. It happens inside relative to something genuinely appreciated and then can be authentically expressed. The opposite of gratefulness is "taking things for granted," an unspoken presumption that resources are unlimited, that magical thinking will work, and the attitude of "leave it for somebody else." True gratefulness is exhilarating, a palpable lightness of the heart at beauty deeply appreciated. It comes with recognizing one's good fortune in the world, now, and perhaps again tomorrow, and whenever else it occurs to you. Gratefulness feeds the soul, enlivens the spirit, and bolsters a life practically, relatedly, and deeply. Can it be found in the talk of this candidate, at least in answer to questions like, "Who do you see as responsible for your success so far in life?"

15. Chastity: Combining Wild Abandon with Disciplined Restraint in Intimate Loving

The early meaning of chastity as keeping control of oneself in the highly emotional experience of sexual attraction, wooing, and mutual pleasuring had a purpose. Sexual pleasure was highly suspected of possibly causing one to get captured by its lure, leading to sexually transmitted diseases (STDs), pregnancy without support, single parenting, dying poor, and indeed, even fears of going to a fiery hell forever.

Though attitudes about sexuality have traveled through many sea changes over the centuries, intimate loving still stands as a true mystery in human living. None of us ever gets it completely figured out. It is a true mystery. Not that we can't know anything about it, but that we can always learn more and never get it all.

Politicians are, at their core, sexual beings, spending some of their human energy focusing on their love lives like the rest of us. But how they deal with the uncontrollable urges of romantic and sexual attraction has serious implications for constituents and, indeed, for the function of the nation itself.

Restraint as a central component of the virtue of chastity has, in many minds, regrettably become its entire meaning. To most people, the word chastity mostly says, "don't." But chastity, in a renewed, expanded meaning, is about doing what it takes to succeed in the spiritual arena of intimate loving and its life-enhancing power. One cannot control that part of life (and all others!) because the evolving world is still full of mysteries, the essence of which we cannot yet thoroughly understand. But virtues help us meet those mysteries with curiosity, enthusiasm, learning, humility, and joy rather than excessive efforts to control, anxiety at its perpetual ambiguity, and depression at its seemingly ubiquitous failures. They help put love and sex together as a major goal and accomplishment in any lifetime.

Chastity cannot be clearly defined but could be described generally as the virtue of *gaining skill, understanding, and lore in pursuing success with intimae loving,* which itself can be described as *two individuals united by mutual attraction, fueled by actively expressed emotional and carnal engagement, relied on for a degree of life satisfaction, and generally changing from early spontaneous enthusiasm to later intentional effort for its subsistence and growing human development.*

There are thousands of books, articles, and most of the songs ever written about this utterly mysterious endeavor that, like all mysteries, can never be completely comprehended. Intimate loving is an entire arena of life, with magnificent recurring energy, almost daily challenges, graceful opportunities, and major changes through its lifetime — from initially 'catching an eye' to tears at the death bed.

As a virtue, chastity serves in a succession of maturing relationships. It helps us all grow up – or not. Most such deeply loving relationships fail, even those that include the confirmation of a wedding. But they compel us to grow in other virtues – tolerance, generosity, patience, interpersonal knowledge and understanding, and even sometimes, wisdom, to gain a bit of life success. At its best, intimate loving calms and supports us in an often demanding and difficult world. But at its worst, it throws us into a chaotic frustration that drains our energy and discourages us in seemingly everything.

Intimate loving, in politics, is even more challenging as it is essentially private but encroached upon repeatedly by public scrutiny without much mercy or understanding. "Looking good" in public does little to feed our private, intimate relationships. But looking bad in this public politics context can damage a career.

The facts are that endless happy romance seems practically impossible to sustain and that the thousands of books and articles written about it eventually fail in the attempt to inject insight into its cultivation and direction. But there seem to be four aspects of it that help keep it alive. Focusing on them helps. They are *enthusiasm, skill, understanding,* and *restraint*. The healthiness of chastity in any individual regarding their current state of romance can be roughly assessed by focusing on these four.

Enthusiasm -The enthusiasm of early romance is classically unique, powerful, and almost irresistible. Enthusiasm is indeed the most attractive quality of all and only partially intentional. When it diminishes into depression, even the pleasurable energy of sexual engagement cannot revive it for long. The dozens of new books written every year can prod its revival by adding new perspectives and strategies to try. But intentionality can only go so far as to inject new energy or return the two lovers to their early glorious excitement with each other. The inclination to find a new partner, one who shows interest, availability, and focused enthusiasm for a man, or the feeling of being enthusiastically and sweetly loved by a woman, is constant for public figures. The politician's contrived public image can be highly compelling to almost any person who is "looking'. That public image, often portraying a person who is successful, physically attractive, and vying for your vote that looks a lot like interest in you personally, seems dreamily delicious and like the enticing "forbidden fruit." Chasing the enthusiasm of youth can be disastrous, and it remains prone to both delight and disaster all through adulthood. That is true "in spades" for many politicians. They can survive infidelity made public, like some of our recent presidents, but not easily and not fully.

Understanding — To feel deeply understood by another person may be the most spiritually invigorating experience of life. To feel that loved joy in or near the context of carnal pleasuring constitutes a peak experience felt by most only for brief periods a few times in life. It is an emotional experience that can only be partially faked. "Emotional connection" has been identified by women as a pre-requisite to enjoying sex and seems difficult to achieve in any regular way by many men. It takes intentionality as well as authenticity of shared emotion to help a person feel emotionally connected. "Working" at understanding a partner along with "spontaneity" sounds like a paradox, and indeed it is. But with practice, it can improve. At some point that combination of intentionally indulging the other and spontaneous responsiveness "now" would be called a major component of the virtue of chastity.

Skill — How to love carnally does not all come naturally. It takes a mutual willingness to be intentionally educated by partners. What a person, woman or man, likes most in lovemaking is highly private. Communicating it to a partner, even one of many years, makes a person extremely vulnerable. Hints help, but they can be misleading for years. Learning what pleasures your partner most and your willingness to provide it is a most exquisite aspect of carnal loving. Most likely, that fundamental dynamic in a couple is universal. It was described even in the Kama Sutra and related Indian writings on optimizing sexual relationships. Skills and a willingness to keep on learning and delicately teaching, as life continually changes the relationship drastically, remain another major component of chastity.

Restraint — The reason for including chastity in this treatment of virtues is that lack of restraint, which is made up largely of patience, fortitude, and prudence, ruins careers and can render groups like churches, universities, and political entities lost in confusion, preoccupation, and incessant gossip, for months at a time. Functionally, such unfortunate improprieties as unwanted sexual advances and marital betrayal can be inefficient and insulting at best and painfully awkward, as well as crippling of the very purpose of politics at worst. Men, in general, learn to live with restraint due to the attraction to the beauty of women that goes so deep in us beginning in adolescence. The fire of that attraction is always just below the surface and so easily slips out in what we see as spontaneous charm beyond mere flirting. That next step to unwanted touch and talk requires intentional restraint that is only learned in many by trial and inevitable error. For Andrew Cuomo and so many others, it can damage or even end a career. Women authors like Susan Faludi (Stiffed, Harper Collins, 1999) strain in their writing to communicate the struggle men feel to negotiate the perceived gauntlet of womanhood in the mostly chaste, endless pursuit of bliss. If there is a female parallel to that scenario, a woman will, of course, need to supply it.

In small assessment group attempts at evaluating character, the virtue of chastity can be addressed by starting with, "Would you be willing to tell us a bit about how your love life has progressed so far? You stay in charge of how deeply you want to share about it. Keep in mind that we believe that the romantic aspect of your life has implications for how you fashion a career in top-level politics. We have lots of time." Follow-up questions and challenges will likely need to be moderated rather than facilitated.

Other questions could be: "Have you ever ended a treasured romantic, loving relationship, or had one ended by your partner?" "What have you learned about yourself and people in general from those events." "Were they only painful life failures or learning crucibles?"

The best-case resultant scenario would be a candidate who can acknowledge that they have gone a bit across the line in pursuing a romance with someone not interested in or legally available for them and are able to talk about what they have learned from that.

16. Peacefulness: Calmly Settled in Confidence, World View, and Accomplishment

A calming presence adds a great deal to the self-presentation of any leader. It probably comes from a personal serenity born of at least a few relatively healthy personal relationships, a developed acceptance of the limitations of human life, and a solid reliance on a positive perspective on transcendence. All three of those sources are invariably difficult to come by. It is possible to fake peacefulness, but not for very long.

Anxiety, as a human phenomenon, is mostly a normal response to an essentially uncontrollable world. Anxiety disorders can be life-confusing, emotionally painful, and can even be fatal. We influence reality; we impede it, cultivate it, and try to shape it. But we don't ever control it at all. And embracing that fact can take a long time to "get." It is a fact, and it is OK. We live in a flow of mystery to which we are invited to respond on a frequent basis on any given day. We influence what we can and flow with the rest. Prayer, in the sense of an ongoing conversation with a positive transcendence, helps negotiate the unpredictability of a day. But it is possible to traverse a quality lifetime without it. It could be that some fine leaders never pray but rather function from a deep sense of non-deist humanism, dedication to the human community, and working in some unique way, mostly joyfully, at improving world living conditions.

A working understanding of spirituality is *how a given person copes with and enjoys what cannot be controlled, including their own physical well-being and behavior, romantic and other interpersonal relationships, the natural world, and the palpable transcendental power above us all.*

A functional spirituality, i.e., the way we care for our own human spirit day to day, supplies a perspective, a purpose, a hopefulness, and motivation for facing whatever we need to for that day. The major religions of the world, at their best, help us do that. The fact that they are often not at their best can be tolerated and then accepted, except when they are clearly destructive to individual people or communities. A peaceful leader, however, does probably need some effective spiritual perspective of their own to stay calm in the context of a day that calls for frequent decisiveness regarding important matters crucial for humanity.

Assessing a candidate's operant, functional spirituality can start with a few queries about that person's religious history, if any. "What has been your relationship with organized religion throughout your life so far?" "What are some of the things you're convinced about regarding spirituality and religion?" "A fair percentage of people have been hurt badly or abandoned at crucial times of their lives by the religious organizations set up to help them. Has that happened to you?" "Will you tell us about that time in your life?" "How did you deal with it?" "Is there a history to your discarding of religion?" "Would you share a bit of it with us?"

"What are some of the ways you nurture your own human spirit now?" "How do you relate to human-made names for transcendent values like God, Allah, Yahweh, and the like?" "How do you think you will deal with the innumerable sources of anxiety you will feel inside when living and working in national leadership?"

17. Class – A Cut Above in Demeanor, Culture, and Savoir Faire

Davy Crocket was elected to the U.S. House of Representatives almost directly from the wilderness of Tennessee. But we are not now in the early nineteenth century. Today, for success in national politics, you will need a bit more class. Subtly rebellious dress, obnoxious demeanor, and crass vocabulary only go so far with an educated and cultured citizenry to be successful in Congress. Elegant self-presentation—in attire, grooming, literacy, and style—signals taking the governing role seriously and being in possession of poise, power, and the appearance of knowing what you are doing, (At times even when you don't!). The advisability for such efforts at culturing a little class in your work may not always have been so important, but it is now, probably even at times for former national class wrestlers and new Pennsylvania senator John Fetterman!

If there is any rudeness from a candidate in public or especially to an assessment group, it needs to be confronted on its function, purpose, and consequences, both intended and unintended. Can this person be annoyed, aggravated, or deeply angry without using crass expressions? Candidates can expect that some people will shower them with invectives and vituperations when they occupy a national office. Can they keep from descending with those people into degrading, early adolescent diction and "acting out"?

Perhaps one day, class will not matter so much. However, how a congressperson dresses and acts affects peers and constituents nonverbally. And sometimes deeply. Fetterman's informal persona may be forecasting a future in which human-to-human communication transcends appearance. But for now, looking shaggy, skanky, provocative, or frumpy can be distracting and even misleading about purpose and attitude. That may not be overriding of substance, but why cause confusing and disturbing sensations?

In the small group assessment context, assessing class could start with, "It has become rather frequent that some congresspersons seek attention in the assembly by being rude and outrageous. How do you feel about that?" "What is your attitude about it?" Efforts at humorous dismissive responses could prompt further comments from assessing group members, like: "What do you see as the value and the limits of usefulness of humor in the assembly?" "Does a pattern of adolescent behavior there indicate anything about the value of a congressperson and their maturity as a legislator?" "Do you think that disruption of the work of Congress is an acceptable strategy in the nation's most revered venue?" "At what point does intentional rowdiness become unjust, even if it is not against House or Senate regulations?"

Someday, research may determine whether the dignified decorum of the U.S. Congress fares better than other national governing bodies, like the often-raucous English parliament.

And finally, "What is a situation in which you wish you could have your words back in criticizing a person, any person, in your work or personal life?" "What did you say that you now regret?" "What was the context?" "What is your attitude about manners and etiquette in conversations among white house staff or congresspersons?" "How important is maintaining both dignity and passion in professional demeanor there?" "How would you contribute to comity and progress in that milieu?

Chapter Five:

A Forum for Challenging Candidates about Their Character

C learly, a person's character is not easily visible except in particularly dramatic, revealing incidents. Ordinarily, the character can remain beneath the surface of our visual self-presentation until it erupts precipitated by events, like when the young unknown is thrust into heroism, saving lives by being at the right time and the right place and taking quick action in a sports arena crowd stampede or at a burning traffic accident. Aspects of character can, however, be "flushed out", as if by a hunter of small game in a field. That hunter needs to get near enough to disturb the pheasant or rabbit for it to bolt from the hiding place. In character assessment, the steps of the hunter are questions put to candidates that unnerve them and compel them to disclose indicators of character traits that ordinarily remain hidden, sometimes even from themselves. As suggested by these earlier chapters, three methods of assessing candidate character can be identified: 1) careful individual observation, 2) large group engagement, and 3) small, process group encounter. The first can begin now for voters by informing ourselves of what characteristics are needed and concentrating on those characteristics as candidates speak in public forums – town halls, formal debates, newsgroup pages, and brief media clips on the various podcast and infotainment presentations.

The second method, large group public encounters, can proceed by media moderators and selected constituents finding better questions that challenge candidates' character in public forums. But that approach will not be enough. It doesn't provide the time and needed opportunity for challenging candidates personally, even confrontation. It was not designed for the kind of in-depth challenge necessary to find character in people. That method will need to be expanded and transformed, as described below, to be adequately effective.

The third method, small process group encounter, will need considerable work over years of transforming election structures before it will become consistently effective. (Chapter Six). Pilot projects could, however, be much sooner.

1. Quasi-Clinical Individual Observation

In the public appearances of candidates, there are two separate perspectives useful for us voters. First, there is the collection of private assessments we make in our own minds about a candidate, shared if at all only with spouses, friends, and in small groups by the water cooler on the job and the bar after work. We follow our thoughts and feelings as we watch candidates speak on TV, at local meetings, and in any other presentations of themselves in their campaign.

We do some of this informal assessment of character now, inside our own private minds. But we could do it far better with more discipline, more reflection, more careful recording for ourselves, and more sharing with one another what each of us sees in the character of each candidate. The appendix of this book is intended to facilitate the improvement of that process. It suggests specific observations to make and offers a format for recording them. These notes can be used in preparation for deciding how to vote. They are your private material shared only at your will.

It may be our obligation as voters to be more vigorous in our character appraisal, as Faisal Hoque has written recently touting transformational leadership in his 2022 book, Lift.

"We all have an obligation to ourselves and others to understand, nurture, and manage the "revolution" that's taking place— rather than having revolutionary change manage us.[xxviii]

Careful observation, a component of personal listening, can be improved with practice. It involves looking closely and listening astutely, both to the content of what a candidate is saying and especially to facial cues and voice clues, which may suggest they strain to say what isn't very true. During political campaigns, and at least a bit before, they are "performing." A voter can intentionally notice the candidate's tones of voice, hopefully sounding more personal than canned, more realistic than idealistic, more genuine than "high-sounding," and overly prepared. Does this person sound fresh or slickly polished, favoring rapid speech that suggests it has been said many times without much emotional connection to the present situation? As one clinical supervisor of mine once suggested regarding my overly analytic perspective on students, "Back off and let yourself know what you know." Overall, what is the intuitive impression you, the listener, get in the conversation, from the pace of speaking, your own impression of their connection to you, fact-checking information (if any) from what they say, attitudes that sound superior (arrogance), resentful (angry without apparent cause), or contrived (e.g., made to sound sad while promoting themselves as having been "bootstrap kids")?

Additionally, are you hearing what you don't want to hear, constituents seeming to understand only one side of a complex issue? Do they rely on jargon, repetitive statements, sound volume, and promises that offer too much, lacking realism? Do they use such strategies that sound conspiratorial, excessively blaming, and "talking past" significant issues and key points? All of these can be indirect clues to a lack of competence or fear of bad reviews looking bad. It could be intentionally sliding over issues or over-focusing on winning rather than talking sense about potentially helpful legislation to consider.

A single negative impression of a voter ought not to be cause for quick discarding of a candidate as a possible leader. But several such impressions combined may push the needle past "not them!" in an assessment.

In medical and health care, a specific kind of listening almost defines the approach to care. It is clinical care, meaning *an approach to assisting people who have major troubles, through direct observation and objective discernment by a calm, knowledgeable practitioner using established frameworks of understanding and, when possible, scientific data from electronic instruments and laboratory tests for diagnosis and prescribing treatment.*

Derived from the Greek meaning simply "bed" (Klinos), the term 'clinical' suggests the need for a bed during serious illness or injury because a person in crisis, even a minor one, may not be able to stand up. When you need a bed for your crisis, it takes a knowledgeable and calm person to remain objective rather than alarmed to care for you. When someone is bleeding profusely, you want someone there who is quick, accurate, and experienced about what to do.

Clinical assessment of more personal and interpersonal problems, however, has been used in psychology, psychiatry, social work, and clinical chaplaincy for about a hundred years. Clinical observation is not foolproof in either medical or personal forms of care. However, it can be used to establish rapport in helping relationships to care for people with mental illness or for rigorous education in the formation of competence in spiritual or social work care. It can also be adapted to assess the character of potential national politicians.

What medical clinicians learn to (mostly) *prescind from* to find objectivity about diagnosis, prescription, and treatment decisions is precisely what person-centered spiritual caregivers need to *focus on* to understand what patients are experiencing *inside* – emotions, concerns, hopes, regrets, worries – and all else that even minor crisis situations can bring to a person. Spiritual (Personal) clinicians stay close to what patients are feeling even more than what they are thinking.

Politicians, in general, seem to stay some distance from their own feelings and even their own best thinking to maintain relationships with party leaders and cling to their special status as well-compensated public figures. What angers them, scares them, saddens them, hurts them, shames them, and even what truly delights them is mostly kept well controlled and often even out of their own awareness. The kind of interaction needed for them to find their own strength of character is quite unfamiliar to them. Being confronted about the hints they give unconsciously about their established virtues may be quite shocking to them, seeming impolite, annoying, and even angering. However, We must know that all those emotional sensations are inside them and can be accessed to some degree by mild and accurate confrontation, a human interaction that can be challenging but can transform key moments.

Assessing character quasi-clinically has both advantages and disadvantages. It requires concentration and objectivity by the assessor, who may not have had serious training in how to stay objective and clearly communicate what they find. That takes skill and practice[xxix]. But just as we typically ponder awhile what may be that sharp pain in our back before we approach the medical care professionals, we can do the same about character. We can learn to concentrate on the indicators of specific virtues in people and identify signs of a serious lack of them in the quiet of our minds.

A clinical perspective differs from a philosophical one. Generalizations about people hold little truth. Globalizing failures and incompetence in any profession – such as "doctors don't listen," "attorneys don't care about the truth," and "'shrinks' are all trying to figure themselves out" – steals the meaning of careful assessment, which is always about this particular person in this specific situation. Philosophizing, in general, about political candidates' character will distract from the value of focusing on what one sees objectively *in a specific* candidate.

Clinical assessment is also different from the kind of pejorative criticism so easy to sink into when talking about politicians. A sort of informal game of who can make the most humorously outrageous negative comments about politicians does not serve the cause of assessment at all. Intentional jokes can be different, as in pointed satire. Humor from them can relieve some of the anxiety of dealing with dreadful situations and even supply a perspicacious grasp that indirectly informs the caregiver about some aspects of the predicament being cared for. How can we tell the difference between healthy humor on the one hand and gallows humor that covers over with jocosity the utter seriousness of really bad news on the other? Most anyone involved can feel it, and it abounds at times in the hospital emergency room.

Spontaneous clinical impressions differ from solid diagnoses, like those we are considering here. Character impressions are mere impressions, using no or few con-validated frameworks of identifying characteristics with precise accuracy. They merely describe what one sees, hears, and intuits. They make our decisions about voting more lively, comprehensive, flexible, and intuitive.

That vigorous but informal approach generates many differing opinions and perspectives, along with their biases and attitudes. Seeking a way to minimize distortions of what one sees of a candidate on TV, a voter could form or join a small group of peer voters to discuss specific virtues of a given candidate, as seen by each group member or a group of them. The form in Appendix One would then be a focus agent to foster the sharing of what each member sees in each candidate.

Large Group Engagement

The second public arena for assessment is done in the candidates' large group gatherings, in person, on TV, or online, which make up much of the drama of political campaigns. As it is invariably configured now, it is not enough, however. Challenging candidates about their character will require new public venues and, eventually, a private one.

At least some minimal engagement between voters and candidates is possible in those venues. Carefully prepared questions asked of candidates typically offer a few occasions for catching indicators of significant character, or lack of it, relevant to voting. It is at those occasions when a select few voters may be able to challenge candidates about their character, as illustrated in Chapters Three and Four.

However, more direct interaction with a candidate is needed. The importance of carefully assessing character requires more direct contact between voters and candidates. A new process for clinical assessment of character, described below, can use the existentialist approach that emanated from the phenomenological philosophy of Edmund Husserl. The essential tenet of phenomenology was that one can never know the *noumenon* of a person or thing, its essential core. One can only know the *phenomenon* of it and how it affects the observer. In speaking to a patient, for example, a personal clinician could not appropriately say, "You are better today." They could only say, 'You seem to be improving", hoping to elicit more disclosure from the patient about their feelings from the patient's own point of view that may be only partially known even to the patient.

In assessing character, then, one can disclose to a person a bit about what one sees in a mildly challenging way, hoping to dislodge more personal experience from the candidate about themselves. Such an approach uses empathic yet challenging questions that are pointed and highly relevant, as well as comments about what the questioner already knows or sees. Feeling the natural interest in what somebody says about you and wanting to clarify it as you see it motivates many people to "say more." That dynamic is essential to careful professional listening and central to person-centered care.

A new process component for improved assessment effectiveness, then, needs to include *confrontation* in public forums now and in small group configurations in the hopefully not-too-distant future. That unique and multi-varied intervention called confrontation at its best radically transforms conversations to a level of greater authenticity and openness, potentially revealing more personal traits than either person intended.

The etymology of the term "confront" "Latin *con*, meaning either "with" or "against," paired together with *frons*, "front," or "face." It means standing face to face, willing to take a conversational course to a deeper level, to a core place in both people involved. It temporarily shreds much ordinary social lubrication and invites a "leveling" with one another[xxx]. We voters need that type of interaction, in some form and venue, with our top leaders before we elect them.

The public interviews conducted by the news media do some of that. But what is needed is a more intentional structure that includes direct challenging on gnarly issues widely broadcast on T.V. The adage, "when a statement is both true and kind, it can change the world," refers to excellent confrontation. "An iron fist in a velvet glove" does the same. Confrontation works best when preceded by genuine conveyed empathy but can be effective even without it.

A proposed format for such a process follows. It would be called:

The Political Candidate Character Assessment Seminar

The candidates, all for the same national office, would first be invited to prepare written responses to one of the following questions, citing statistics and relevant publications as they wish. On the day of the seminar, they would gather to speak in turn on the assigned topic for ten to fifteen minutes on national T.V. Only two minutes of extra time is allowed. The microphones are turned off quickly for violators.

A small panel of interviewers (two or three) would then query them in turn about their presentations and challenge them about the attitudes, stances, and underlying virtues that seem to be disclosed in them. The following describes how eight such topics could be the substance of the eight sessions, one a week for eight weeks.

Week 1: How do you understand the various components of the "unsheltered wanderer" phenomenon currently frustrating almost all of our major cities? How do you see the complex causes

of that situation? How do you feel about that entire phenomenon? And how do you see current policy, budgeting, and programming contributing to that worsening situation?

A bevy of different follow-up questions would be asked by a small panel of interviewers, which is made up of two media personalities and two ordinary constituents savvy to the terminology and concepts of character. In this first session, the audience and commentators would be charged with listening and forming follow-up questions that focus on finding in each candidate a developed sense of fairness, the virtue of *Justice*. Does this candidate possess at least a sliver of justice in them, as shown by their attitudes, values, and assumptions communicated in their preparatory writing and orally during the seminar? Most importantly, can the interviewers and TV participants detect the feelings of hurt or aggravation in talking about the pain in the lives of any of the wanderers or anybody else being treated grossly unfairly? The questions in Chapter Three of this book suggest directions and pointed challenges for this discussion. Is there a justice issue here regarding the other side of privilege? What are the pieces missing in the makeup of some of the particular wanderers who have never had a chance in life? How does this candidate feel when observing these unfortunates up close? Have they ever seen themselves contributing to this problem at any level? How do they feel about that?

Week 2: Please write and talk seriously about your own strengths and weaknesses as a person, a spouse, and a lawmaker. Will you illustrate your assertions about yourself with examples from your past personal and legislative history?

Here, the observers listen especially for indicators of the candidate's *humility*, a reasonably accurate appraisal of their own person. They will especially notice indicators of hyperbole, minimizing, pomposity, and efforts at humor, which could be blurring the awkward directness of talking about themselves. How solid does this person appear "in their own skin"? Are they fooling themselves about their own importance? Are they wimpy about their own strength, influence, and bearing?

Week 3: Will you describe a situation or event in which you learned as a child or an adolescent that the truth is sacred, never to be easily violated? How do you see a top politician's role in countering the current erosion of truth-telling in marketing, broadcasting, political wrangling, social media, public education, and possibly AI? Will you confess in a story of how you have failed in telling a truth, obfuscating a reality, dodging an obligation, or escaping a responsibility in childhood, adolescence, young adulthood, or politics that was destructive to your image or would have been if known? What was your experience during the time of the so-called Big Lie of 2020-2021 and its fallout? What do you hope you would have done as a congressperson at that time?

Participants are listening for indicators of *integrity,* a solid habit, and conviction about telling the relevant truth as much as possible. Additional queries for follow-up can be found in Chapter Three under integrity. These include pressuring a bit on how they feel about the Big Lie in politics in recent years.

Week 4: Please describe a bit about your history of using courage and strength in standing for one of your solid values against difficult opposition in the public arena. What values are you proud of standing for, either publicly or indirectly, in your previous career?

Participants and observers are listening for *fortitude* indicators, times in which this candidate was criticized for boldness during their expression of a stance that was controversial. Follow-up questions address any previous work they have done standing against something that they believed would hurt the common good. Then, they continue with questions like, "Have you ever been in a physical fight? For what value? Have they ever stood solidly for a value and been defeated? How did you feel about your life path of 'going against' something that once cost you dearly? How do you feel about that now?"

Week 5: How do you understand both sides of the abortion conflict long-simmering among us in this country? Please avoid

taking your stance on the question until you have commented on your knowledge and understanding of both sides.

Participants and observers will be paying attention to the *political savvy* of this candidate, the combination of knowledge, understanding, and wisdom needed by political leaders for negotiating highly complex chronic issues in which not every constituent can have their way. Questions that continue confronting the candidate on their knowledge and understanding of why so little is ever done to help the situations of women complexly pressured by the intense love of their infant on the one hand and the financial and personal burdens of raising a child in their unique situation. How do they feel about those women and the few men who are also caught in that bind? What would they do to care for the children involved who now must live in a situation of poverty due to the sacrifices made by their loving mother?

Week 6: How would you describe the difference between a king, an emperor, a president, a legislator, and an executive director? Which do we need most as top leaders in our country and why? Which fits you best?

As described in Chapter Three, people attending are listening for any signs of dedication to humanity and political savvy. Is this candidate most motivated by party politics, clinging to an important political position, or otherwise self-benefitting from the public decisions intended to serve as many constituents as possible? Is there a hint of altruism in this person, an almost idealistic urge to selflessly care for their constituents, their country, and even more importantly, the world community?

Week 7: How can you describe both sides of the U.S. gun rights dispute with its geographical complexities, child safety issues, and seemingly intractable polarization components? Do top political leaders have a role in facilitating dialogue to maintain the basic rights of all sides, with increased clear limitations in each of those rights? What are your ideas about moving forward with that issue in which groups continue to cling to their individual rights in

apparent intoxication with their autonomy and fears of losing it on one side and the welfare of people trying to live in peace on the other?

Observers are looking for the virtues of *dedication to humanity, knowledge, understanding, and humility,* hoping to hear a bit of new wisdom from somewhere. Is this candidate ready to spearhead venues for facilitating dialogue between thousands of individual people face to face with one another, voicing and discussing their intense positions on this complex and volatile issue congenially?

Week 8: How serious do you see the alleged world climate crisis? Why do governments, including the U.S., seem so slow to address it vigorously? Can you speak clearly and eloquently about what actions you think are needed from all of us to "save the planet"? How urgently? What is the role of legislators and other officials to provide perspective on this gnarly issue? What is the role of individual citizens? How would you attempt to influence people on this vital, existential issue?

Here, participants and observers are listening for indicators of *thrift* (assiduous care of resources), *knowledge, and understanding* of the concerns on both sides of this issue, furthering productivity on the one hand and "saving humanity" on the other.

Participants and observers are asking themselves how each candidate seems *to be feeling* regarding specific aspects of the vital world issue of climate change and whether they would be ready to champion that cause. Would they, for example, sponsor face-to-face discussions among leaders of each side? That could be a key to the effectiveness of this conflicted project. With some exceptions, emotions tend to be left out of these conversations or at least unrecognized or unmentioned. They must be made a major factor in people seeking to assess the character aspects of these candidates. Where is the wisdom of devising specific actions that are needed inside the homes of all of us so we can visualize just how it would be if we all took this issue seriously?

*   *   *   *

The third method for engaging a candidate about their character is the subject of the proposed small, process group future of character assessment described in Chapter 6. Throughout this book, we have listed questions and the types of observations that elicit character indicators. However, there is no venue dedicated to character assessment, a place, time, or structure dedicated to engaging candidates directly and persistently. Chapter Six shows how small groups could provide that arena for confrontation and education about the character of potential candidates.

Chapter Six:
The Future of Political Character Assessment - Small Group Encounter

Small groups of similar yet diverse individual members with savvy leaders have always, or at least for 50,000 years, been valued for their influential power. Tribes, squads, teams, ensembles, gangs, and professional partnerships have added effectiveness to accomplishing tasks, power to the weakened, enjoyment to work, and integrity to defining truth, quality, and openness in recent decades.

The twentieth century brought on a new level of development and use of the small group to promote interpersonal growth, clinical education, and healing of personal and interpersonal ills. What has been learned in those groups can now advance the assessment of character. Group richness is highly adaptable to very diverse tasks, from support groups and work groups to university faculty boards, committees, and task forces. Now, in a well-led dynamic form, it can facilitate the process of making reasonable assessments of the character of candidates.

Something uniquely different happens when groups of five and six people sit for a significant amount of time closely facing one another to pay attention to each other's inner processes and interact as objectively as possible about them. The dynamics of the group – the conglomeration of the ever-changing emotional flow within each member – and among them affects them all in a shared experience that may be seen differently by each member, with moments of synchronicity in which all agree with what they see. That exceptional situation is an advancement in the evolution of humanity that can be facilitated by experienced leadership for focus, clarifying interactions, and specific pockets of learning. It has been a major innovation in collaborative learning that began maturing in the twentieth century.

As character assessment in the public forums of political campaigns becomes more established in national leader elections, it will become possible and feasible to develop processes for another level of character assessment in *confidential small process groups of educated and well-prepared constituents*. Hopefully, the motivation for such a collaborative, *confidential* project as a part of political campaigns will be strengthened as its benefit is seen in assessing character in *public* events for better-informed voters for elections.

There is no small group format and tradition of assessing the character of political leaders. It would need to be invented, but not from scratch. Successful small group processes developed during the twentieth century serve as examples of how such groups have a way of getting to the soul of group members. Something about a small space and the faces of six or fewer members, in immediate proximity that, beckons forth more self-disclosure than most any other context. The unique dynamics between people in small groups are designed to pay attention to what is happening emotionally among them, challenge all present to participate, and expert leadership can channel that impetus into deeper relationships than social, academic, or work groups developing independently.

Three highly successful small group movements stand out as exquisitely successful in addressing specific painful human situations during the twentieth century. None of them perfectly fits the purpose, i.e., finding excellent or adequate national leaders. And indeed, such groups do not "work" for everyone. But all three of these described below resulted from painful human needs and catalyzed discoveries that used the power of small group dynamics to address current problems underneath. They are: 1) AA-based addiction treatment, 2) clinical pastoral education, and 3) group psychotherapy. If you have not been present to and seriously engaged in any of these movements, you may see them as boring, trite, and of questionable value because they are all seen as designed for somebody else.

All of these were initiated by professionals caring for people in difficult, sometimes excruciating physical or interpersonal pain. All have successfully improved the relief from such pain by using small group dynamics. None of the three are useful in themselves for our present purpose of assessing politicians' character. But they all include using essential virtues, albeit with different names, for their unique purposes of assessment of character for improving painful lives. Combined, they show ways of assessing virtue in small group formats that fit the need.

Creating a system of such small groups, initially for character assessment and eventually for maintenance of collaborative government relationships, can eventually catch the governing bodies up with the functional level citizens need for them to have to forge new policies and systems for the benefit of the people.

Addiction Recovery

Alcoholics Anonymous (AA) started itself in the mid-1930s, made up of long-term dunks meeting in a cafe after attending spiritual-seeking groups at a Manhattan church.

Each in uniquely tragic deteriorating lives, they were desperate to get into sobriety and stay there. They were accustomed to desperation after an average of about twenty years skidding along in the fog of drunkenness and, long ago, tiring of it. Incredibly, they discovered in conversing informally that they were staying sober for the first time in history that anyone knew about. A jolt of insight revealed that their ability to not drink at all a day at a time was not due to the church meetings. It was because of what was happening among them having coffee in their café groups after those meetings!

In discussing what they were doing over coffee that was working, led by Bill Wilson, a frustrated alcoholic stockbroker, they began to coalesce the various stories of their drinking pains, distill what was happening in the café meetings, and fashion into words what seemed to be common elements of their path to sobriety. These statements, haggled over for months and word-smithed extensively, were eventually termed the Twelve Steps of Alcoholics Anonymous. The originators had passed together their experiences and memories of the interactions that seemed key in their recovery path. In a few years, there were over a million people learning to live without alcohol one day at a time, using those steps together in small groups in this country and several others. The basics of their group interaction in the café have great relevance for assessing political candidate character.

A treatment model based solidly on those principles was later designed, primarily by psychiatrist Dr. Nelson Bradley, counselor Dan Anderson, and chaplain Gordy Grimm, at Willmar State Hospital in Minnesota in the 1950s.[xxxi] Its center moved to Hazelden, MN, at one point, which became a familiar name for the best of addiction treatment.

The treatment process continued to develop there, featuring guiding, challenging, and confronting victims of alcoholism to work the steps, not just recite, memorize, or even understand them. Working the Steps was a painful and arduous set of tasks. Rather than merely learning about them, discussing them, and getting insight into the process of recovery, it took investment, vigorous interpersonal engagement, radical honesty, and most of all, enormous courage of action to authentically work them, partnered and nudged by ex-addict counselors and savvy chaplains. It still does.

Particularly relevant here is that, while using very little classical virtue language, such treatment groups and the more common recovery groups of A.A. itself base their responses to members seeking sobriety on such growing characteristics as humility, honesty, openness, gratefulness, fortitude, and prudence. The traditional virtue words like prudence and fortitude are generally replaced by colloquial words (good sense, guts, and stopping "stinkin' thinkin'," for example). But the meaning is the same and powerfully understood. Counselors are accustomed to using those points of view in their caregiving because many of them have seen themselves tortuously gaining them as a habitual practice in their own recovery paths. Counselors who work that way are experts at assessing such commonly uncommon traits because they are essential to maintaining their own recovery lifestyle and, indeed, thereby staying alive. Such counselors and experienced ex-addicts could do the same self-explorative guiding with a bit of further training for individuals intending to seek national political office.

Alcoholics Anonymous treatment groups are distinct from AA itself. It is the difference between climbing a mountain peak with a few untrained and inexperienced buddies on the one hand and doing it with a half dozen other fit and steady individuals, including a guide who "knows the ropes" on the other. There is massive power in small groups, but here, it is enhanced by counselors observing, validating a person's positive efforts, and challenging their complex conscious and unconscious resistances. The life, recovery, and process experience those counselors have amassed could show a way to recognize the virtues needed by politicians, too.

For example, nobody recovers from addiction with a tone of grandiosity still pervading their speech. That is quite observable to the experienced eye and even to similarly defeated, struggling peer addicts. Recovering alcoholics have all been humbled, and some embrace that humility – that clear awareness of both their enormous worth and their human limitations. That experience is not merely cognitive. In fact, very academic people can have more trouble stumbling to recovery than those with minimal education. Gaining humility in any adult without it takes a radical experience, not mere academic learning.

We must acknowledge the tight limitations of self-disclosure of Alcoholics Anonymous, in part because it is a violation of treasured humility not to do so. The AA community does not speak for any causes, claim to make people healthy, or solve personal problems. It helps them stop using alcohol and do whatever it takes to stay sober today. Addicts are not necessarily elegant people. But they are far more capable of a normal life than they were while drinking and generally gain considerable consistent virtue in the process.

Honesty comes along with humility. Most of them started drinking as teenagers, and as adolescent drinkers, they had to let go of telling the truth long ago. Drinking was illegal. They had to hide it for that and other radical reasons. From shading the truth to bold-faced lying, they would say anything for a drink. Now, it turns out, if they shade the truth even a little, they put themselves in critical danger of taking that first drink and starting the plight all over again, like they always have before. Recovering alcoholics tend to be starkly honest. They cannot afford to lie, even a little, and they know it. In the famous TV series West Wing, some of the most admirable characters eventually turned out to be in recovery from alcoholism. Developing the openness, understanding, gratitude, and healing interpersonal regrets and resentments that drag the human spirit down (forgiveness and gracefulness) is never as simple as it may sound to people who do not have alcoholism illness.

Character assessment groups can be patterned somewhat like AA treatment groups (not true AA groups) designed and facilitated to focus on the key personal characteristics, some known for centuries to be necessary for quality leadership of governments. Counselors trained and experienced in AA treatment methods could be useful in designing and helping to conduct groups confronting potential political candidates about essential virtues such as humility, honesty, openness, gratefulness, fortitude, patience, and prudence.

Clinical Pastoral Education

Clinical pastoral education (CPE) originated gradually about ten years before AA, in the 1920s. It, too, uses small group dynamics to challenge, support and educate. It is now essential preparation for individuals who want to work as professional spiritual clinicians (deeply educated both academically and clinically) and chaplains in facilities such as hospitals, mental health programs, prisons, and hospices. Such students need academic preparation, but even more importantly, they need at least a year of the small group interactions of CPE dedicated to experiential education, learning from experiences of engaging patients with a "listening first, non-anxious presence" and lingering attentiveness approach that hears about the patient's predicament from their point of view and how it has already affected their lives.

The education for professional chaplaincy then centers on that chaplain talking extensively and openly in the peer group setting about their thoughts and feelings during the patient conversation. The group members agreed to offer that one chaplain direct feedback and challenge about how they cared for the patient, how it affected that group member emotionally, and how they might next time care even better. That learning process also uncovers for everyone who engages it authentically, relational habits, patterns of communication, and character defects that inhibit the authenticity and empathy of their caregiving work.

As group members, they are led by an experienced clinical educator who focuses them on the relevant experiences of the group members relative to the member presenting the case. They come to expect one another to relate with direct feedback, growing authenticity, courageous openness, human understanding, interpersonal fortitude, and an exquisite brand of conveyed empathy. They will need all of that when helping very troubled people in deep need in the public institutions of this country.

Some of the highly trained and certified leaders of CPE groups, called certified clinical pastoral educators, could similarly be employed to participate in small groups to assess candidates for virtues needed in readiness for national office. They could eventually lead some of the character assessment groups when those groups develop. (Chapter 6)

CPE shocks almost everyone who enters it, even though they may have heard about and read about it extensively beforehand.[xxxii] The Initial formation of the group speaks loudly that this is a place for authenticity, for direct feedback to one another, for challenging each other's self-perceptions, for engaging one another's troubling personal issues, and for ineffective patterns of interpersonal relating. Group members take time to look closely at bits of communication that are passed by in social interaction but may be troubling and inhibiting in patient conversations about painful living and immanent dying situations. CPE doesn't make people perfect at all. But it renders them far more helpful to people in the most difficult times of their lives.

Just as AA developed in New York and Akron, Ohio, CPE was developed out of a need for better, more personal care of some of the sickest people in the state psychiatric hospitals and then general hospitals of New England and various other institutions across the eastern U.S.[xxxiii], then the southeast, and the upper Midwest. Still little known to the public even today, its Association for Clinical Pastoral Education (ACPE) accredited programs continue to boast the best, most challenging kind of life-transforming small group experiential education there is. Benefitting from it requires some character strengths to start with and is almost sure to build more of them into anyone who qualifies and invests themselves in its programs. The ability to communicate directly, human to human, with integrity, openness, interpersonal courage, and occasional wisdom are some of the fruits of successful CPE[xxxiv].

A program like CPE could be built and eventually required to prepare interested people for national political office. There is, of course, a long path to establishing the parameters and functional organization needed for such a process. Nevertheless, voter pressure could go a long way to prodding state election boards to eventually use some of the dynamics of CPE to sort out those applicants for candidacy who show at least a beginning level of character as evinced by observable key virtues from those who don't.

Group Psychotherapy

Several people-helping professional pioneers are credited with developing structured ways of helping people with mental illnesses (that includes many of us at some point in our lives) and others in painful life situations in small groups during the twentieth century.[xxxv] Now small, therapy groups, support groups, or process groups are innumerable, designed to optimize the identification of troubled people with one another in professionally intimate interaction to help one another cope with their identified concerns. Groups now are conducted for a host of problems and relational issues so diverse in their purposes and adaptations that they cannot even be listed here. And they need not be. What is salient is to describe some of the aspects of small groups that are universal and adaptable to the character assessment of public figures.

Sigmund Freud's writing[xxxvi] on using psychoanalysis in small groups was the first to harness that configuration of four to six members for healing and learning about oneself. He did not persist in developing that tack of working in groups. However, during the twentieth century, several theorists and practitioners did. In a remarkable acceleration of the evolution of therapy and growth groups the size of an average family of origin, they made a striking contribution to the evolution of humanity. They were developing a basic process and understanding of small groups in general, from which most of the successful change and growth groups, grief groups, recovery groups, and clinical learning groups have been grafted. Therapists of that century were beginning to recognize the power of personal change that small process groups generate.

Such groups set up a culture of authenticity and expectations of engagement of both emotions and cognition intertwined. They are not the same as discussion groups, academic seminars, or think tanks. The difference is huge. Small process groups engage the emotions of members, their struggles, their personal and interpersonal concerns, their relationships with one another, and even their pathological limitations of communication that can be improved.

There are numerous styles and theories of conducting therapy groups and even other types of groups in which people learn and grow. Therapy groups, in general, require members to choose to participate because they have significant painful issues that are burdening or preoccupying their lives. That is not generally the case with candidates for election. Therapy groups are not directly appropriate for character assessment. Neither are AA groups or CPE groups. But elements of all three can be adapted for that specialized task.

Picture a group of six constituents as described above, prepared previously to process interaction about character. A leader, perhaps with a well-prepared partner, begins the session with a few well-chosen words that introduce the milieu as focusing on emotions combined with thinking, the importance of meaning what you say, the value of direct feedback to see how others are seeing you, and bringing focus to the overall task of assessing the character of the candidate present.

No type of group session is designed for six people focusing therapeutically on one person for several hours at a time, even PhD dissertation presentations in which the interaction is almost totally cognitive. All of these need to be altered considerably to address the character assessment task.

Hearing candidates talk extensively about themselves will remain an initial group task, the importance of which cannot be minimized. Some, maybe most candidates, are not accustomed to talking personally about themselves directly for very long. Their political success has hinged on their talking about problems, policies, stances, and how their party exceeds the value of the other one. Their self-presentation has not featured much personal disclosure that was not previously staged. Essentially, they have been selling themselves, much like addicts. But character appraisal requires catching them describing themselves freshly and saying more than they planned to say about themselves; for some, that will be more than they have ever said about their values, feelings, relationships, attitudes, and basic assumptions in life.

After that relaxed beginning, the group leaders could use a simple task of naming the various virtues one at a time and open the floor to the whole group to probe the candidate, and then shift to another virtue while one member keeps notes. One group member could serve as a "presenter", read written material previously prepared by the candidate, and offer questions based on the reading to focus on the issues in question.

In any case, experimentation would be necessary at first, and what is learned by assessing early candidates could be used to improve those that follow.

It could be expected that the experience of a day of assessment would change almost every candidate in major ways. Process groups established as virtue evaluators, even if as brief as one day of sessions, would promote interpersonal learning of great value to politicians' work as well as grist for the mill of uncovering virtue strengths and weaknesses. Facing a prepared group of six highly interested and virtue-savvy constituents of various disciplines and walks of life who are challenging them about their convictions, histories of political experience, and specifics of their human development would be an unforgettable day. Everyone involved would benefit, except for a few who possess too much virtue deficit.

That single four to six-hour day would also expand the candidate's *relevance to constituents*. It seems easy for some top officials to brush aside constituents' expectations and preferences on how they conduct themselves. How do they almost ignore their voters in favor of maintaining close allegiance to a few political party leaders? Or do they even hear such concerns amidst their accustomed entitlement, superior material benefits, and the traditional honor bestowed on them? Here, in this group, candidates or members of Congress up for re-election would soon be treated as if they were partners of constituents, invited in close proximity to explain some of the reasons for their congressional positions and decisions. It would become clear in some instances that their own beliefs about issues are not what motivates them most in their voting in Congress, and that may not feel so good to them when put in bold relief in a small group. On the other hand, we can predict that some candidates would make new connections to savvy constituents, in some cases generating satisfying feelings of collaboration and lasting appreciation.

Chapter Seven:
Building Structures for
the Assessing Work

W hat would a quasi-clinical process to privately evaluate the always subjective aspect of character in the language of virtues in our national leaders look like? For now, picture, for example, a group of five or six experts in various diverse fields led by a professional small group facilitator or two. An assessment group must be small, and one of the seven members begins to be large. It is easier to hide in a large group. Four is too small, except when unavoidable.

The assessing members must be common citizens, albeit educated to a degree that makes them likely to be moderately successful in American society. Perhaps a policeman (one respected by their peers); a teacher (a prize-winning one); a military veteran (with combat time); a member of Alcoholics Anonymous (sober for a while); a high school or college instructor of political science or history; and a psychologist familiar with group psychotherapy. They are about equally divided between men and women, perhaps with a gay or bisexual person or two among them, and there is some race and age diversity visually evident, as well as sometimes some observable disability. They are dressed as if it is a casual Friday. The group will have been instructed basically about virtue as a language of character, with hints at how to recognize it in its various forms. They have read this book and liked its themes. They have worked together a bit on recognizing and eliciting candidate disclosures in stories about elements of their character. They have seen the report form, a bare three pages, like the one in this book's Appendix, which was designed for individual private use but eventually revised to negotiate better the line between privacy rights and the public's rights to know their top leaders in some depth. Group leaders need to be highly familiar with process groups and have worked as group leaders in some versions, such as those in clinical pastoral education, AA-style addiction recovery, or group therapy. They may have a partner present with similar expertise. These two ask the first questions and see that any required questions get asked. They end the session but only after the group has been active for about four to six hours, not including breaks.

Group assessing members bring their own biases, mostly consciously acknowledged ones, and have learned to consider them as preferences and opinions. They do not necessarily know one another, but they are all from the same state or province, probably where they volunteer as group assessors.

In reporting on the assessment experience, the group members will strive for a clinical description of the candidate from their character's perspective. As a necessary component of psychological interviews and clinical pastoral education courses, a clinical report here means a *carefully objective narrative based on direct, face-to-face observation of interpersonal interaction and described with con-validated frameworks of understanding people,* in this case, the language of virtue. CPE educators, group therapists, and professional psychologists of almost any experience will be familiar with how to begin writing these, a skill that will develop over time. The level of participation of a particular candidate and their willingness to be assessed will vary from bare compliance if their participation has been mandated, on the one hand, to eagerness to share if it has not.

The written report will become, for some candidates, a valuable badge of collaboration with the political system. For others, it will become a detriment to their career. Who manages the reports? The issue of walking the line between candidates' right to privacy and the state's right to know who the citizens are electing will need to be negotiated and set in writing. Who, for example, will be able to read the report? What are the parameters of the report? Who keeps confidential records over the years, if indeed any need to be kept?

Once voters get accustomed to the idea of seeing the character as an important aspect of candidate selection, further structures can hopefully be tried. Establishment, for example, of "assessment tanks" in the vein of "think tanks" in which members will exchange ideas, methods, approaches, coordination, procedures, record keeping, and discussions about the value, the "how-to," and the limitations of assessing character. Perhaps every state will establish a "character assessment board" whose mission is to prepare people for candidacy by education and small group experience and to manage the assessment process for that state. Some states may choose an "assessment Czar" to organize, administrate, evaluate, and periodically revise the system.

Beyond these basic initial parameters, each state organization will design its own rules and regulations for functioning in that state. People familiar with political science in general, and the election mores in each state in particular, will someday finish this chapter.

The group session could end briefly, without much explanation, rationale, or prediction of future events. The group leader simply says something like:

Thank you for taking part in this exercise. We will write a brief narrative report on how we assess your relevant character traits at this time in your life and either, for example, (It will be made available to you and anyone registered to vote in the United States") or (… made available to you and then filed in the confidential office of the state elections authority).

Perhaps the greatest challenge in this entire project will be to oppose the politicization of the assessment process constantly. People accustomed to considering everything as a fight against something else will have a most difficult time even living within established structures. Continually working to defeat those sidetracks into blame of another party, over-influence of party leaders on party members' congressional voting, and excuses for not looking directly or talking clearly about key issues could prove very difficult at first. The group coordinators would need to carry powers of dismissal of group members for cause.

Chapter Eight:
Can Character Be Grown
in Congress?

A future congress, cabinet, or government department could benefit from a system of voluntary, regular, small character-enhancing groups established for processing their part in the unique, constant interactions and relationships among legislators. The goal would be to free to some extent, their political deliberations and maneuvering from some of the underlying interpersonal conflicts and communication habits that impede decision-making. As Congress, for example, is gradually made up more of people with a collaborative spirit, openness to interpersonal processing could grow. The use of such a system would increase the authenticity, collaboration, and dedication of group members, one by one, to the essential work of the various components of government. It would augment the character of some legislators all the way through their terms.

We may be accustomed to seeing the character as bequeathed to us at birth, or at least in early development—as if, as an adult, "you either have a positive character or you do not." But small process groups may have changed that. The kinds of personal transformations that take place in members of well-led process groups can be life-changing and often are. The character can grow. A few of the concepts that have emerged in the small group movement may lend substance to the idea of congressional small groups.

Engaging, for example, means, in this context, addressing one another with the assumption that emotions will be open for exploration as well as relationships among group members. Engaging another person means speaking directly to them, asking pointed personal questions, listening carefully to one another, and describing bits of how they see one another, both their first impressions of one another and then how they see and feel about one another functioning in the group itself. Giving and receiving direct feedback from one another will be a major feature of the group interaction, especially about how they see one another in the present moment and the group's history.

In small process groups, dynamics quickly get "personal" in ways that discussion groups don't, a central purpose of joining them.

Processing means *taking time and making space to look closely at the thoughts and feelings of members relative to any interaction between them or between one member and the total group.* When one member, for example, says something of direct importance to another, all members may have observations, opinions, feelings, and thoughts about that interaction. When one member, or the leader, requests processing that initial interaction, the group work is to understand that initial interaction more clearly from several points of view, especially about the motivating emotions lying beneath the observable surface of those group members involved. Interpersonal processing is the stuff of group learning and often healing as well.

In the small process group, the skills of *initiating personal engagement, offering direct feedback, clearly conveyed empathy, identification with another,* and *empathic confrontation* form a cluster of dynamics known to generate rich interaction found only rarely anywhere else. For those who volunteer for the group membership and are ready for it, the result is a human-to-human group connection that transcends the social lubrication, incessant "selling," image management, and unconscious maneuvering so common in ordinary social conversation, and even political and academic circles. The small group, with faces so close and body language visible, invites more "leveling," a direct sharing of what is essential about the current immediate interaction beckoning towards collaborative relationships.

Some growth benefits of such volunteer participation in confidential groups would likely be:

Practicing interpersonal collaboration — As a regular active member, weekly or monthly, a congressperson would be experiencing collaboration in a striking new way. They would be seeing one another in a mixture of vulnerability and strength, a human-to-human relationship rather than a competitive ones. As each of them identifies genuine goals for themselves in the group, they quickly are compelled on some level, to be of help to one another rather than shun them as adversaries. That is the universal human experience when earnest people are in close proximity to one another with even a smidgen of goodwill in them. They may even occasionally feel the satisfying feelings of successful collaboration and hopefully be influenced by that experience. The facilitator asking each group member for their written evaluation of one another's group performance through maybe an eight-week segment of time, and then processing each member's written evaluation out loud in the group would be an additional fruitful challenge. It is an almost universal component of excellent CPE programs halfway through the typical three-month programs.

Improving objectivity –- Becoming more descriptive than judgmental, especially in writing, matures a person's perspectives, something that would benefit many congresspersons. Learning that skill of description helps crowd out the highly judgmental habits that seem to abound among congresspersons, though often veiled by polite Southern phrases such as "No offense but…." or "I hate to say this but…," or "The (young or old) gentleman…." Conveyed empathy and prescriptive confrontation can flourish among such developing habits. And dualistic partisanship fades with those six congressional peers' faces so visible and near, weekly, for an hour or so, for several weeks.

Increased Personal Integration–- Being in a confidential room with an expert facilitator and a diverse group of peer legislators for an hour or several sessions will challenge the personal protective shell typically placed and maintained around legislators. New relationships can emerge in that small group, in which all participants seem more human to one another, more candid, more trusting, and more able to converse about important political issues and how they affect them personally. If that milieu infects the self-protective, overly cheery, or sadly dour attitudes of some ambivalent group members even a little, it will begin to eat away at the ways candidates tend to use strategy and image management rather than their own genuine thinking and emotional experience in their work.

More generally, active participants of ongoing process groups, like any of the three described in Chapter 7 above, tend to learn and grow even with minimal expert facilitation. In treatment programs, for example, there are usually grief groups to help ameliorate the effect of major losses on patients' efforts to stay sober. Often, in a group of eight patients, a few will say nothing for the entire hour. In the daily evaluation sheets, patients fill out at the end of the day, those silent members were frequently the ones who named "grief group" as the high point of their day. (Indeed, there is a fabled AA saying that you could lock 30 alcoholics in a barn for 30 days, and 10 of them would come out and stay sober for the rest of their lives due to the sharing that would occur among them!)

Irvin Yalom, one of the early writers about group therapy, in his seminal book The Theory and Practice of Group Psychotherapy, describes some of the primary benefits that accrue from vigorous participation in small process groups. A few of them constitute functions that could be useful for creating such groups to further the personal growth of congresspersons. They refer primarily to groups that function for several meetings and are made up of a number of peers and one or two leaders. Like AA and CPE group cultures, these benefits contribute some insight into how small groups function as highly different from large groups like local communities, church congregations, modest crowds, and business conferences on the one hand, and two-person dyads like parenting, pastoring, managing, counseling, and friending on the other.

They are presented through this author's interpretation to adapt them to the congressional setting project. Only the paragraph titles are directly from Yalom.

First, process group experience almost always *instills hope* in serious participants. For example, hope is often starkly visible on the faces and in the voices of people in group treatment for whatever constellation of problems they bring to the group. The atmosphere of that group setting of ordinary people opening up about their lives becomes a healing milieu. That place of the stark honesty of troubled people seems like it changes something in their brains. The observed hopefulness in those group settings, though it most likely won't last without feeding it somewhat consistently for a while, is one indicator that when people talk directly and honestly about themselves, even a bit, they emerge from meetings feeling just a little better. A single small group session where people talk openly about themselves can alter the direction of a member's life. It will not heal them, fix everything about them, or change their employment, bank account, or family. But they see one another's faces, catch their tones and accents, and can be moved by their unique lives, somehow similar yet uniquely different from their own. They are relatively happy doing what the newbie has seldom been able to do: smile about their day at its end.

Second, Identifying and Empathizing— Sitting down in a small group of diverse peers conversing openly about themselves puts a person in touch with what is common about all of us humans. We all eat, need to work, feel some love, and are looking for more, and bring our styles of relating and patterns of communicating with us wherever we go. Group members are quickly and quietly touching what is lost by physical distance – the *universality of human beings.*

If a person is quietly feeling isolated, then courageously speaking some personal truth in a group will invite connection with at least some of the co-humans around. It is far easier to bad-mouth a person from afar than one with whom you will be sitting in a circle, equidistant from the center, for a few hours with a leader both facilitating and moderating to promote significant depth of interaction. We humans are all more alike than different at our core. Process group experience eats away at feelings of conscious or unconscious superiority that underlie racism, agism, sexual bias, and classism, especially if you may be asked to talk about those feelings in that group. Beneath the reality that some are more privileged than others in various ways, in that group, for now, there is a distinct impression that everybody is of equal worth. That substrate will almost always eventually emerge in the group interaction.

Third, Imparting Information—

Small process groups are not made specifically for instruction. But they do educate in both bold and subtle ways. As members talk about themselves, others hear the stories, experiences, and facts conveyed. Shared experiences optimize the likelihood of identifying with one another, increasing the virtue of understanding people different from oneself and those one has known so far in life. It also increases the likelihood of unearthing the *altruism* that lurks somewhere in the hearts of (almost) all people. If the customary haggling of politicians' interaction is suppressed in a process group, some of that healthy information seeps into the personality and personal history of some group members, imperceptibly affecting their interpersonal behavior ever after. In short, when group members experience a peer member getting sharply jolted by negative feedback for acting like a jerk, they are less likely to act that way themselves.

For example, if a group member sees hints of pain in another member, they are far more likely to take it seriously, feel compassion, and move to support, even if they've seen the same thing in a large group from the same person. Proximity of faces brings hearts closer. It awakens altruism, at least enough to mess with a heart-mind mechanism that has become repeatedly biased. Facial proximity doesn't heal people automatically. But it makes prejudice a bit uncomfortable in all except the most hardened bigots. Prejudice is a pre-judgment. When the heart is able to intuit for itself, in physical and emotional proximity to another human being, it no longer is quite so tied to what they have been automatically judging negatively before, in prejudice.

I was continuously amazed when listening extensively to one addict after another, at a time near the end of three weeks of treatment, as they completed a "Fifth Step" of the famous Twelve Steps of Alcoholics Anonymous. That is a one-to-one session with a chaplain (or another trusted spiritual leader) near the time for discharge, sharing in detail the "exact nature of our wrongs," the worst of what they remember having done to people, and the wrongs done to themselves by others. After two to three hours of well-prepared, often teary, sharing their worst regrets and wounds, I'd always ask something like, "OK. What is the positive side of you? What do you have going for you?" Invariably, their thoughtful response started with some form of, "Well, I like people." Presumably, most hadn't felt that way all their lives, but three weeks of intensive treatment groups had etched into them an appreciation of the humanness of people and the hidden natural inclination to help them.

Fourth— *The Corrective Recapitulation of the Primary Family Group* can easily be missed even in therapy groups. It is what Yalom called the way in which dynamics of our family of origin that get unconsciously repeated in our group behavior can be pointed out by group members or the leader for reconsideration and possible change or healing. We have all been shaped by our family of origin, and if asked, we can recount what was our primary role in the family when it was assembled. In every small group, and even some larger ones that we become part of, like work groups, we tend to unconsciously re-create that ingrained family group and, in some strange way, repeat our original group role. Process groups, in particular, offer a chance to improve on that repetitive pattern, healing a bit the sharp corners of your style of coping with and enjoying that family. This can happen even without the process being seen. But when it happens boldly, other group members invariably feel a bit better about themselves and –their colleagues.

Fifth–the *development of socializing techniques* is somewhat similar. According to Yalom (among many others), besides our family of origin, we are shaped in youth by the feedback we get from all kinds of people to whom we substantively relate—teachers, classmates, pastors, coaches, aunts, uncles, cousins, and serendipitously some strangers. The look on their face when they engage us, the patterns of attitudes people seem to show when they see us, and the words they use to describe us all tend to socialize us and help us fit uniquely into society.

Such socialization is missing in many unsheltered wanderers—basics like combing your hair, bathing, hydrating, eye contact, and a dozen other fundamental behaviors that help us get along in a quite dysfunctional society. How all their painful relationships have bent them personally is never known. Nobody listens to them long or carefully enough to find that out. Crisp feedback in a process group, however, can teach very basic social skills instantly with such comments as, "Wow, Ms.! That sounded and felt rude." Brief silence. "Does that matter to you at all?" It is sad to say that sometimes, recently, such a comment might fit the political milieu.

Sixth and finally – Imitative Learning) — *Imitative Learning* — There is also what group members can learn from imitating the group leaders and other group members. Seeing one group member artfully and unpredictably cleared from past resentments for considering collaborative relating to another by group processing, heartfully complement a former adversary; or fill holes in a group member left there from their family of origin are examples of what Yalom called *Imitative Behavior*. That is *learning from watching and seeing actively in a peer member the value of a better way to interact, behave, and live among people in society.* What is largely absent from people living on the street, for example, can be learned somewhat by interaction in a person-oriented group (though mental illness, combat experience, rape, and incest require specially led groups as part of effective treatment programs (which are only rarely available or accessed by combat veterans on the street.) Candidates for office are probably sometimes touched by the virtuous behavior of a peer with solidly observable virtue, like prudence, fortitude, and class. That recognition would be able to show up boldly in consistent small group interaction.

Improving the overall mutual understanding and identification among lawmakers and thus the familiarity and respect with which they relate can improve their collaborative work. Greater personal enjoyment of the role and life satisfaction can only follow.

Appendix:
A Beginning Recording Sheet for Character Traits

This form is intended for private use to record a voter's impressions of candidates' character traits for top political office while or after that candidate has finished one or several public presentations. The content of this form could, of course, be shared at the will of the recorder or not. Parentheses on this form indicate a probable absence of that virtue.

The centralizing question is, "Does this candidate exhibit in personal history, disclosures, personal self-presentation, or large group engagement, substantive indicators of specific virtues such as:

1. Justice –- A basic sense of fairness

Apparent visual or spoken verbal discomfort at hearing concrete examples of serious physical or social injustice.

Candidate tells a story about how they have worked with enthusiasm for obtaining a bit of justice for anyone (person or group), but themselves.

Yes_____ Somewhat_____ No_____ No Impression_____

2. Humility – Relatively Accurate Self Appraisal

Talks extensively about themselves relatively accurately, including both personal assets and limitations, without hyperbole, minimizing or excessive goofy humor.

Calmly acknowledges awareness of the specifics of their strengths and limitations as a person and maybe as a public figure.

Apparently, they are calm and confident in their thinking and values as they talk about themselves.

(Thoughtless hyperbole, minimizing, or hyperverbal obfuscation)

Yes_____ Somewhat_____ No_____ No Impression_____

3. Integrity–- A habitual pattern of telling the relevant truth.

Tells a story of how they learned to reverence telling the truth as children or later.

Tells a story of suffering the pain and damage wrought by their own direct or indirect lying.

Yes _____ Somewhat_____ No_____ No Impression_____

4. Dedication to Humanity – A basic inclination to contribute to the evolving human race.

Talks cogently about world hunger and their attitude about it A Basic Inclination to Contribute to the Evolving Human Race

Does this candidate have a hint of dedication to eventual global community?

(Signs of hyper-nationalism)

Yes___ Somewhat__ __No___ No Impression_____

5. Fortitude: Strength with courage for actively addressing current conflicting issues or threats

Tells a story of how they have shown verve, courage, and strength as a leader.

Gives an example of what would motivate them to confront a peer politician about errant behavior, individually or participating in communal intervention.

(Inability to address the idea or history of their own fortitude)

Yes____ Somewhat____ No____ No Impression____

6. Temperance: Moderation of attitude, anger, avarice, appetite, and alcohol

Talks (apparently) openly about at least one, preferably two excesses to which they are prone and how they have struggled with them.

(Persistently denies any difficulty with excess, perhaps minimizing hidden concerns.)

Yes____ Somewhat____ No___ No Impression____

7. Benignity – Consistently seeing the good in situations and people.

Does this person strike you as reasonably approachable?

Does this person warm up as you engage them? (Or interpersonally withdraw?)

(Are you inwardly suspicious of this person?)

8. Charity and Kindness in the moment

Shows intentional kindness to a present person known to be emotionally hurt.

Uses a gentle, soft voice –one in an efforts to convey–- empathy.

Yes____ Somewhat___ No__ No Impression____

9. Counsel: Authentic use of consultation from peers or other experts

This candidate is clear about whom they follow, admire, and from whom they elicit help.

This candidate can narrate the most recent time they asked for help.

Yes____ Somewhat____ No___ No Impression____

10. Savvy: Combining knowledge, understanding, and wisdom

This candidate shows a wide and deep understanding of diverse people and has used decisive action that uniquely fits a person's needs in a difficult situation.

Demonstrates considerable understanding of at least a few diverse constituent groups.

This candidate listened carefully and personally to some group members today.

(Seemed obtuse to complexities of differing cultures.)

Yes____ Somewhat____ No_ No Impression____

11. Thrift: A realistic perspective on resources

Talks openly about the history of their personal financial thrift.

Talks about their historical considerations for using economic caution with public resources.

Yes____ Somewhat____ No____ No Impression____

12. Prudence: Patience and Poise with Circumspection

Maintains composure under pressure, with elegant bearing, reserve, and intuitive circumspection.

Consistently remained composed and eloquent during their campaign and this assessment hour.

Yes____ Somewhat____ No____ No Impression___

13. Tolerance and Acceptance: Bearing failure and aligning with fate

Talks openly about major disappointments in their career.

Identifies a significant regret or resentment they have effectively faced in their own behavior.

Yes_____ Somewhat_____ No_____ No Impression_____

14. Reverence: Awe at What is Beyond Us

Can this candidate talk cogently about their history with religion?

Can they talk about how they currently nurture their own soul?

Can they talk genuinely with substance about their gratefulness?

Yes_____ Somewhat_____ No_____ No Impression_____

15. Chastity: Elegance in enthusiasm, skill, understanding and restraint in love-making

Could this candidate openly and substantively rate their love life and its history?

Did this candidate, with either solemnity or humor, reveal at least two things they have learned from engagement with romantic lovers?

Can this person acknowledge ever slipping "over the line" of sexual appropriateness?

(Have they ever been convicted or accused of sexual harassment or abuse?)

Yes_____ Somewhat_____ No___ No Impression_____

16. Peacefulness: Calmly settled in confidence and accomplishment

Can this candidate share their experience with anxiety? Can they talk seriously about what they are proud of so far in their life?

Yes_____ Somewhat_____ No_____ No Impression_____

17. Class: A "Cut Above" in demeanor, culture, and *savoir-faire*

Does this candidate physically affect you positively, in appearance, etiquette, aroma, personal pace, and charm?

Yes_____ Somewhat_____ No_____ No Impression____

Acknowledgments

S everal people weighed in on the contents of this book as I was writing it. The most influential were Robert (Bob) Popovich, John Gillman, Sandra Walker, Dale Walker, Wes McIntyre, Julie Bradley, and Charles (Chuck) Ahlgren.

Bob's professional identities, formed by decades as a chiropractor, clinical pastoral educator, and, for a time, a Dominican Catholic priest, coalesced with his natural and practiced ability to describe people in clinical writing to make his critique of the text and style of the manuscript invaluable in shaping it. John, a clinical pastoral educator and university professor of world religions, was great at suggesting further resources, and at pointing out bold assertions, I tend to make without enough documentation. Chuck, who spent his adult life in the U.S. Foreign Service and teaching at the U.S. Army war college, was most helpful in expanding my awareness of some early writing of our nation's founders, some more recent books that address convictions similar to those presented here, and for soft critique of my tendency towards idealism.

I am most grateful for my stalwart supporters, Julie Bradley, Sandra Walker, and Wes McIntyre, who managed to stay positive about my writing no matter what. Dale Walker's natural and studied cynical side toned down my optimistic, even sanguine tendencies towards a little better balance.

My Mom and Dad, both deceased for over forty years, had meager education but made sure I got far better schooling than they did, with considerable financial stretching for them at the time. They showed me virtue and character, though they never studied it. The experience of loved, lovingly critical individuals with solid character goes far deeper than books, teachers, and professors shape us.

But I am grateful too for those instructors in Catholic education, from my first grade through graduate school. There are a lot of things still out of shape in Catholic culture, but I'm glad the Reformation theologians did not completely root out the virtue traditions of Catholicism as putting too much power for salvation in human hands. Virtuous living makes the world better, even if it may not be beneficial after death. And that is especially true of leaders of all kinds, top political ones in particular.

There was a jivy young African American man working as AA coordinator at Presbyterian St. Luke's Medical Center in Chicago in 1974, whose last name was Byrd. For him, I will always be indebted. He befriended me and, for almost two years, took me to dozens of closed AA meetings where I didn't belong, in various places in the city, just at the time I was stirred to learn in-depth about that stark world of recovery that formed in the 1930s. That and his interpretations of 'how it works' taught me what I needed to experience about that incredibly powerful atmosphere and the unique ways basics of the AA way of life for learning the heroic virtues that were helping them stay sober. That experience broadened my understanding of spirituality far beyond the religious concepts with which I was raised, giving me an initial positive direction in life. The tone of this book, as deeply humanistic, with reverence for the human value of religious ideologies, was further cultured there.

Most important, however, in supporting me, was my wife, who for each of my books, too often gets left waiting as I write. She has been as tolerant as anyone could be, a sure sign of a unique brand of resilient love beyond what anyone could want.

This is a short book. You can read it all in a few hours. If reading it improves anything about how you vote, I think it was worth the writing time. The country, democracy, and the world need thoughtful voters who are sensitively cognizant of the character of those they elect. Eventually, we will establish a small group process in each state to do the necessary assessment of character, thoughtfully, directly, courageously, and well. I believe we will evolve to that.

Notes

[i]Humanism as dedication and service to the human community and betterment of every human being's life situation and living conditions, in both its Deist and non-Deist forms.

[ii]Sarah Chayes, Thieves of State: Why Corruption Threatens Global Security (2015, W.W. Norton and Company, New York.)

[iii]Federalist No. 57, in Federalist Papers, Seattle, Amazon Classics. 2017.

[iv]Those would include the Sumerians, Egyptians, Chinese, Mayans, and inhabitants of the Indus Valley: northeast Afghanistan to Pakistan and northwest India.

[v]An old Babylonian dialect in which the Code is written.

[vi] Hilsman, G. J. Hilsman. Intimate Spirituality: The Catholic Way of Love and Sex. (Rowman and Littlefield: 2007), Lanham MD.

[vii]The Analects, a chief source of understanding the basics of Confucius's teachings, should not be expected to satisfy a Western theoretical mind. There is a simplicity in the writing that led to great confusion among splintered groups in several countries over many centuries, like that of Christianity in its conflicting forms worldwide. The rendition of the basics of Confucianism presented here is taken from commentaries, the extrapolations of this author, and Wikipedia.

[viii]There are now many lists of the Fruits of the Spirit due to complex circumstances in which they have been taught over centuries.

[ix]That term "evangelical" has now been highly co-opted as referring to spoken rigorous belief in Jesus Christ in a trans-denominational coalition with zealous members in several different large Christian Churches. Its only association with the evangelical counsels mentioned here is that they both refer in name to the Christian gospels.

[x]Bernard of Clairvaux, <u>Sermons on the Song of Songs</u>, vol. 1, 2.

[xi]Bernard of Clairvaux, <u>The Steps of Humility and Pride</u>, M. Basil Pennington OCSO (Liturgical Press, 1989. St. John, MN)

[xii]Pierre Teilhard de Chardin, 2004, The Future of Man. Ch. 5, The New Spirit, pp. 74-88, (Image Books: New York, N.Y.

[xiii] Along with Martin Seligman in that early movement there were Chris Peterson, Rollo May, James Bugental, and Carl Rogers.

[xiv] Seligman, Martin and Christopher Peterson, <u>Character Strengths and Virtues</u>, American Psychological Association / Oxford University Press; 1st edition (April 8, 2004).

[xv]This process, "action/reflection/further altered action", is characteristic of learning in Clinical Pastoral Education – try something that makes sense in caring for a patient, reflect on it communally with a group of peers and a clinical supervisor, and then try something else incorporating what you learned from the first try.

[xvi]Michelle Maiese and Heidi Burgess, "Types of Justice," *Beyond Intractability,* Eds. Guy Burgess, and Heidi Burgess. *Conflict Information Consortium, University of Colorado, Boulder. Posted: July 2003 <http://www. beyondintractability.org/ essay/ types-of-justice>*

[xvii]Cf. Yaqeen Institute, "More than Just Law: The Idea of Justice in the Koran," February 7, 2020.

https://yaqeeninstitute.org/read/paper/theidea-of-justice-in-the-quran, accessed November 9, 2022.

[xviii]Jason Gregory (2014). <u>The Science and Practice of Humility</u> (Inner Traditions: Rochester, VT).

[xix]Isaiah 11: 2; such words as "power" and "might" are used by different translations.

[xx]House of Cards was a political drama TV series lasting from 2013 to 2019, featuring ruthless intrigue at every turn.

[xxi]Plato, Op. Cit, Book 3.

[xxii]Plato Op. Cit. Book 4

[xxiii]Galatians 5

[xxiv]See Chapter Two, Isaiah, about this early list of virtues in the Hebrew Scriptures.

[xxv]Ibid, Christopher Peterson and Martin Seligman (2004).

[xxvi]Dennis John Kucinich, Proposed H.R.2459 — 107th Congress (2001-2002). "Establishes in the Department the Intergovernmental Advisory Council on Peace, which shall provide assistance and make recommendations to the Secretary and the President concerning intergovernmental policies relating to peace and nonviolent conflict resolution." Congress.GOV.2002

https://www.congress.gov/congressional-record/volume-148/issue88/house-section/page/H4078-4079. Accessed September 5, 2022.

[xxvii]Chayse, op. cit., pp. 6, 67-77.

[xxviii]Faisal Hoque, (2022). Lift: Fostering the Leader in You Amid Revolutionary Global Change. Fast Company Press (no street address), call 800.501.9571 ext. 2225.

[xxix]Gordon J Hilsman, (2016) Spiritual Care in Common Terms: How Chaplains Can Accurately Record the Spiritual Needs of Patients in the Medical Record. Jessica Kingsley Publishers, London, and New York.

[xxx]Gordon J Hilsman, Confrontation in Spiritual Care, An Anthology for Clinical Caregivers, Summit Bay Press (Olympia WA: 2022) pp. 3-17.

[xxxi]Commonly called the Minnesota Model of Treatment.

[xxxii]Gordon J Hilsman (2018) How to Get the Most Out of Clinical Pastoral Education: An ACPE Primer, Jessica Kingsley Publications, London and Philadelphia.

[xxxiii] The several histories of the clinical pastoral education movement include those by Edward Thornton (1970), Charles E. Hall (1992),

Joan Hemenway (1996), Steven King (2007); and Sean J. LaBat (2022), among others.

[xxxiv]Like colleges, law schools, and medical schools, CPE programs can vary in quality. For this writer, the best known are the programs accredited by the U.S. Department of Education, by what is called the Association for Clinical Pastoral Education.

[xxxv]Kurt Lewin and Carl Rogers were two of the earliest, in the mid-1940s. Samuel Slavson, Lou Ormont, and Irvin Yalom are a few of the better-known initiators. There are others.

[xxxvi]Freud, Sigmund, <u>Group Psychology, and the Analysis of the Ego.</u>

[xxxvii]James Strachy, trans. The International Psychoanalytic Association, #6 January,1967.

Index

www.ingramcontent.com/pod-product-compliance
Lightning Source LLC
Chambersburg PA
CBHW052114030426
42335CB00025B/2971